SAMUEL JOHNSON

Book Reviewer
in the
Literary Magazine: or, Universal Review
1756–1758

THE

Literary Magazine:

OR,

UNIVERSAL REVIEW:

For the Year MDCCLVI.

Teach me, ye Muses, your devoted Priest,
Whose Charms with holy Raptures fire my Breast,
The Ways of Heav'n, the wandering Stars to know,
The radiant Sun and Moon's Eclipses show,
Whence trembles Earth, what Force old Ocean swells
To burst his Bounds, and backward what repels;
Why wintry Suns roll down with rapid Flight,
And whence delay retards the lingering Night.

VIRG. GEORG. II.

VOL. I.

LONDON:

Printed for J. RICHARDSON in *Pater-noster Row.*

SAMUEL JOHNSON

Book Reviewer
in the
Literary Magazine:
or, Universal Review
1756–1758

by
Donald D. Eddy

Garland Publishing, Inc., New York & London
1979

Library of Congress Cataloging in Publication Data

Eddy, Donald D
Samuel Johnson, book reviewer in
the Literary magazine, or, Universal review, 1756–1758.

Includes bibliographies and index.
1. Johnson, Samuel, 1709–1784—Knowledge—Literature.
2. Literary magazine.   3. Book reviewing.
4. Criticism—England—History—18th century.
I. Title.
PR3537.L5E27   820'.9'006   78-53000
ISBN 0-8240-3425-2

Printed on acid-free, 250-year-life paper
Manufactured in the United States of America

To
Edie

with love and gratitude

Acknowledgments

This book was developed slowly over many years and is largely bibliographical in nature, so its author now stands indebted to a host of librarians and antiquarian booksellers, friends and colleagues. The investigation started with the writings (and later assistance) of the late Professors Allen T. Hazen and James L. Clifford of Columbia University. I am very grateful to Professors Donald F. Bond, Arthur Friedman, and Gwin J. Kolb of the University of Chicago, with special thanks to Gwin for reading and correcting several earlier versions of this text. I also thank Dr. J. D. Fleeman of Pembroke College, Oxford and Mrs. Donald Hyde of Somerville, New Jersey.

In the course of writing this book (and pursuing the manuscripts and books of John Brown), I have visited scores of research libraries — indeed, the count is now more than one hundred — so necessarily I must extend a general note of gratitude to all those who have been so generous with their time and assistance. At many libraries I have not visited personally, I am grateful to staff members for answering my telephone calls and letters and for sending so many Xerox prints. I hope it will not be considered invidious if I select a few librarians to thank personally by naming them: Mr. Ian Willison of the British Library; Mr. Robert Rosenthal of the University of Chicago; Miss Alexandra Mason of Kansas; and Mr. N. Frederick Nash of Illinois. At Cornell University I thank especially Miss Marcia Jebb, Mrs. Caroline Spicer of the Reference Department, and Mrs. Jane Woolston of the Department of Rare Books (who deserves special credit for her patience and helpfulness). At the Beinecke Library — and earlier, in the Sterling Library — at Yale, I am grateful to Mr. Herman W. Liebert for sharing his knowledge, his enthusiasm, and his fine personal collection of books. Also at the Beinecke, I extend special thanks to Miss Marjorie G. Wynne, who is simply the best librarian I have ever known.

I am deeply indebted to many antiquarian booksellers for their knowledge and assistance, especially Robert J. Barry, Jr., John R. B. Brett-Smith, Ralph T. Howey, Bryan Maggs, and Stephen Weissman. Above all, I am grateful to the late Michael Papantonio of Seven Gables Bookshop; if this small volume in any way conveys a genuine love of books, it is due largely to my years of friendship with Mike.

I thank the British Library for allowing me to cite information in the printing ledgers of William Strahan; also, the Bodleian Library for allowing me to cite information in the paper stock ledger of William Bowyer.

I thank Miss Elizabeth Cadman of Cambridge for typesetting this

[vii]

book in eleven point Baskerville with twelve point leading on an IBM Selectric composer. The small caps are nine point Baskerville. The pages were then photographically reduced approximately ten per cent.

I thank Cornell University for several sabbatical leaves, and I gratefully acknowledge receipt of several Humanities Faculty Research Grants. I thank Cambridge University for awarding me the Munby Fellowship in Bibliography for 1978–79 and I am grateful to Darwin College, Cambridge for their hospitality during that time.

Finally, a book that developed as slowly as this required special efforts of patience and sacrifice by my wife, and I am most grateful. She is the only one to whom this book could be dedicated.

D.D.E.

Cornell University

Contents

Acknowledgments   vii

Abbreviations of works frequently cited   x

List of illustrations   xi

Preface   xiii

Chapter I
Johnson's Contributions to the *Literary Magazine*   1

Chapter II
The Books Johnson reviewed for the *Literary Magazine*   29

Chapter III
Johnson's Techniques as a Reviewer   79

Notes to Chapter I   95

Notes to Chapter III   103

Appendix A
The *Literary Magazine* and the *London Chronicle*   107

Appendix B
Chronological List of Books and Pamphlets   127

Index   143

ABBREVIATIONS OF WORKS FREQUENTLY CITED

Bloom   Bloom, Edward A. *Samuel Johnson in Grub Street.*
Providence, Rhode Island: Brown University Press,
1957.

Life   Boswell, James. *The Life of Samuel Johnson, LL.D.* . . .
Edited by George Birkbeck Hill and revised by L. F.
Powell. 6 vols. Oxford: Clarendon Press, 1934—50.

Courtney   Courtney, William Prideaux, and David Nichol Smith.
A Bibliography of Samuel Johnson. Oxford: Clarendon
Press, 1925 [reissue of edition of 1915].

Greene   Greene, D. J. "Johnson's Contributions to the *Literary
Magazine.*" *Review of English Studies*, 7 (October, 1956),
367—92.

Hazen   Hazen, Allen T. *Samuel Johnson's Prefaces & Dedications.*
New Haven: Yale University Press, 1937.

LM   *The Literary Magazine: or, Universal Review.*
London, 1756—58.

LC   *The London Chronicle: or, Universal Evening Post.*
London, 1757—1823.

Illustrations

I.   Title-page of the first volume of
     the *Literary Magazine*   *Frontispiece*

II. John Wilkie's apology in the
     London Chronicle of June 16—18, 1757   *Facing page* 13

III. John Wilkie's new plan of the
     Literary and Antigallican Magazine
     in the *London Chronicle* of January 21—24, 1758   108

The frontispiece is reproduced through the courtesy of Herman W. Liebert. Plates II and III are reproduced with the permission of the Syndics of Cambridge University Library.

How many books and pamphlets did Johnson review throughout his life? The answers to this question will vary considerably among serious students of Johnson depending upon their degree of acceptance of the many attributions made in scholarly articles since World War II. This lack of precision seems inherent in the murky field of attributions: some are proposed with great confidence in the strength of the external and internal evidence, while others are proposed tentatively and with slight evidence. This work is no exception and presents attributions of both varieties.

However, even a scholar who is sceptical and conservatively inclined would probably agree that Johnson reviewed approximately sixty items and that a majority of the reviews were published in the *Literary Magazine*. This alone is ample justification for studying the magazine, a study made even more appealing by remembering that Johnson's best reviews — such as those on Jenyns, Hanway, Byng, and Warton — are all contained in the magazine.

I originally intended to include in this book a discussion of Arthur Murphy's contributions to the *Literary Magazine*, but as the material grew I realized that it would have to constitute a separate work. I believe that Arthur Sherbo's *New Essays by Arthur Murphy* (East Lansing: Michigan State University Press, 1963), in spite of its many merits, does not go far enough in establishing the canon of Murphy's journalistic writings in 1757—58. Much of the material — especially book reviews — in the *Literary Magazine* of 1757—58 shows Murphy's hand; in fact, indications of Murphy's authorship are present to such an extent that I believe it is very probable that Murphy assumed Johnson's responsibilities after he left the magazine. I certainly agree with Sherbo that Murphy was writing fairly regularly for both the *London Chronicle* and the *Literary Magazine* in 1757—58. Some of the same people were involved in the two periodicals both as publishers and owners (see Chapter I, below) and certainly the *London Chronicle* was used in many ways to try to bolster the lagging circulation of the *Literary Magazine* (see Appendix A, below). So far as I have been able to determine, Arthur Murphy is the only writer known to have been contributing steadily to both periodicals during these two years. (Except for the introductory essay to the first number of the *London Chronicle*, January 1, 1757, Johnson is not known to have contributed anything to the newspaper during this period.) It seems highly probable, therefore, that Murphy was the writer responsible for adapting material for the newspaper from the magazine (and vice versa) and for making knowledgeable comments about it. Several of my later comments (particularly in Chapter I) are based upon this assumption, which remains unproved here.

I had also intended to include as appendices bibliographical accounts of the John Douglas — Archibald Bower controversy and the Admiral John Byng controversy. In this book I argue that Johnson reviewed four of the Douglas — Bower tracts and five of the pamphlets relating to Byng. However, since the large majority of the publications in both controversies were not reviewed by Johnson, I was persuaded not to include those accounts in this book.

This book is intended to be a companion to the three volumes of the Garland facsimile of the *Literary Magazine* (constituting a fourth volume of commentary, so to speak). I have therefore condensed this book considerably by excluding many quotations from the magazine.

Two notes of correction must be made about the Garland facsimile edition. (1) Some copies of volume II were issued in which plates numbers 10, 11, and 14 were inadvertently misbound. Fortunately, the plates are tipped in so that that accident may be corrected easily; the correct locations of plates are listed at the beginning of volume I. (2) In my bibliographical introduction in the first volume, I list only volumes I and II of the *Literary Magazine* as being in the library of Queens' College, Cambridge. I am now delighted to report that in another part of that library, in a bound volume of tracts, there is also a complete copy of volume III. Collation shows that all pages are present and in excellent condition in all three volumes; volume I lacks plates numbers 3 and 5, and volume II lacks plate number 8. It is thus by far the most complete run of the magazine in any library today.

* * * * *

This work has prompted inquiries from friends as to reasons for the delay in publication. Johnson, in a letter to John Taylor dated November 18, 1756 [Chapman no. 106], gives a good answer:

> There is one honest reason why those things are most
> subject to delays which we most desire to do. What we
> think of importance we wish to do well, to do any thing
> well, requires time, and what requires time commonly
> finds us too idle or too busy to undertake it. To be idle
> is not the best excuse, though if a man studies his own
> reformation it is the best reason he can allege to himself,
> both because it is commonly true, and because it contains
> no fallacy, for every man that thinks he is idle condemns
> himself and has therefore a chance to endeavour amendment,

but the busy mortal has often his own commendation, even when his very business is the consequence of Idleness, when he engages himself in trifles only to put the thoughts of more important duties out of his mind, or to gain an excuse to his own heart for omitting them.

Addendum

How did Jonas Hanway distribute copies of the first edition in quarto of his *Journal of Eight Days Journey* . . . London: H. Woodfall, 1756? The book was issued privately instead of being published, but most copies are unsigned and not all copies are dated by Hanway in manuscript on page 361 (see below, pp. 65–66). In later years Hanway became known for his signed, presentation copies in handsome and unusual bindings which he designed; but for this book — presumably before he was having his works specially bound — he used an engraved paper slip which he addressed and signed. Here reproduced, with the kind permission of the Master and Fellows of Pembroke College, Cambridge, is the slip loosely inserted in the first quarto edition of Hanway's *Journal* in the Pembroke College library (shelf mark 34.18.1), a copy not otherwise signed or dated by Hanway. The size of the plate is 4.8 by 10.0 cm., while the entire paper slip measures 7.2 by 19.0 cm. It is printed on normal book-paper stock with chain lines and no watermarks, but all four edges of the paper are gilt!

Miss Burford may possibly be "the good-natured sensible Miss B******" mentioned by Hanway on page 13 of the *Journal.*

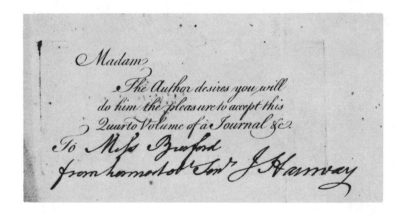

CHAPTER I

JOHNSON'S CONTRIBUTIONS TO THE *LITERARY MAGAZINE*

I. Introduction

The name of Samuel Johnson is so frequently associated with eighteenth-century newspapers, magazines, and book reviews, that it is somewhat surprising to realize the extent to which they originated and developed within the space of Johnson's life. When Johnson was born in 1709, Samuel Buckley's *Daily Courant* was the only daily newspaper published in London, and it had started only in 1702 (*CBEL*, II, 708). Johnson was a young man of twenty-two the year Edward Cave initiated the *Gentleman's Magazine*, the first magazine published in England which managed to survive more than a short time. Yet as early as 1731 (according to the introduction to the first volume of the magazine) newspapers were "so multiply'd, as to render it impossible, unless a man makes it a business, to consult them all." It adds the statistic that "upon calculating the Number of News-Papers, 'tis found that (besides divers written Accounts) no less than 200 Half-sheets per Month are thrown from the Press only in London, and about as many printed elsewhere in the Three Kingdoms." In fact, at least five newspapers were flourishing in London by 1731 (*CBEL*, II, 710, 717).

However plentiful the newspapers and magazines were, the book reviews in them suddenly were made to seem insignificant with the first appearance of Ralph Griffiths' *Monthly Review*, a monthly octavo of about eighty pages devoted solely to book reviews. The advertisement for the first issue of May, 1749 states, in part:

> When the abuse of title-pages is obviously come to such a pass, that few readers care to take in a book, any more than a servant, without a recommendation; to acquaint

the public that a summary review of the productions of
the press, as they occur to notice, was perhaps never more
necessary than now, would be superfluous and vain.[1]

Evidently the public agreed that such a periodical was necessary, for
it was quite successful and continued publication until 1845.

Although many magazines began their publication in London in
the 1750's,[2] the only one which presented real competition for the
Monthly Review was the *Critical Review*, the first monthly issue of
which was advertised in February, 1756 (although covering the
period from January 1) and was published March 1, 1756. It was
"printed for R. Baldwin," and its first main editor and director was
Tobias Smollett. It, too, was successful and continued publication
under that title until 1817.

Interest in periodicals by no means centered in the book reviews.
The reading public was large enough to support various types of
periodicals, and several which were inaugurated in the years 1756–60
received contributions from the pen of Samuel Johnson. Among these
magazines and newspapers are the *London Chronicle*, the *Universal
Chronicle*, the *Public Ledger*, and – of primary interest here – the
Literary Magazine: or, Universal Review.

It is difficult to determine exactly the identity of all the men
associated with the *Literary Magazine* when it was started early in
1756. Perhaps most trustworthy are the accounts of John Hawkins,
who was a good friend of Johnson's and at this time also a member of
the club which met at the King's Head in Ivy Lane, and of Arthur
Murphy, who worked with Johnson on the magazine. Murphy says in
his biographical account of Johnson that the *Literary Magazine* was
started "under the auspices of the late Mr. Newbery . . . ."[3] Hawkins,
in his *Life of Samuel Johnson*, says that "one Faden, a printer, was
the editor" of the *Literary Magazine*.[4] If this is true, then William
Faden worked on the magazine in a triple capacity, for he was probably
the printer of all twenty-seven monthly issues as well as unquestionably
being the publisher of the first nine issues – i.e., all of the first volume.[5]
The next ten issues (numbers X–XIX) were published by J. Richardson,
and the last eight were published by John Wilkie.[6] Griffith Jones, a
friend and business associate of John Newbery, was probably a contributor to the magazine, although no specific items have been attributed to him.[7] Robert Chambers, of Lincoln College, Oxford, presumably
made some contributions to the magazine;[8] and Arthur Murphy himself is the source of the statement that the review of Burke's *Sublime
and Beautiful* "was written by Mr. *Murphy*, and given, with many
other pieces, to the literary magazine . . . ."[9]

Many of these same men were allied in other journalistic projects

in the same decade. Newbery may have been a financial backer of
the *Rambler* for John Payne,[10] and he probably financed the
Universal Chronicle for Payne in 1758.[11] Robert Dodsley, Newbery
and his business associate Benjamin Collins, as well as J. Richardson
and his partner William Innys, were probably original partners in
founding the *London Chronicle*, which started publication on
January 1, 1757.[12] In 1760 Newbery was responsible for starting
the *Public Ledger* (Welsh, pp. 40—44). William Faden was closely
associated with Newbery throughout the decade: he was the printer
of the *Rambler*, the *Literary Magazine*, and the *Public Ledger*; and
in 1760 he was the publisher of some issues of the *Universal
Chronicle*.[13] Griffith Jones and John Wilkie were long associated,
Jones as the editor of the *London Chronicle* and Wilkie as its publisher.[14] Jones was also the editor of the *Public Ledger*.[15]

Nor were these their only journalistic activities. Newbery, for
example, owned a share of *Lloyd's Evening Post*, and he also started
the *British Magazine* in 1760.[16] John Wilkie was the publisher of
several periodical essays during this period: *The Herald; or, Patriot
Proclaimer* was published in thirty weekly numbers from Saturday,
September 17, 1757 through Thursday, April 6, 1758;[17] and the
Bee was published on eight consecutive Saturdays in October and
November, 1759.[18] Wilkie also became publisher of the *Lady's
Magazine* in 1759.[19]

What seems to emerge from these facts is the picture of a publishing
"syndicate" —a small group of men who combined, perhaps informally,
to finance, edit, print and publish quite a number of periodical publications in the 1750's and 1760's. Strahan and Dodsley were peripheral
members of the group — in fact, they seem to have united with the
other members only in the *London Chronicle*.[20] However, Newbery,
Payne, Faden, J. Richardson, Jones, and Wilkie were all deeply involved in several different periodicals.[21]

Various writers were employed by the group, usually (I assume) by
Newbery. Certainly two of his favorite authors during the 1750's
were Christopher Smart and Samuel Johnson. Arthur Murphy's
periodical essay, the *Gray's-Inn Journal*, was printed by Faden,[22]
and Murphy wrote for both the *Literary Magazine* and the *London
Chronicle*.[23] Beginning about 1759 Oliver Goldsmith and Tobias
Smollett assumed significant responsibilities for the "syndicate" both
as writers and editors.

Our concern, however, is with Johnson, whose business association
with Newbery began at least as early as 1751. On April 18 Johnson
wrote to Newbery to borrow two pounds; on July 29 he borrowed
a guinea, "for which I will account to you on some future production";

and on August 24 he asked for another guinea, "for which I shall be
glad of any opportunity to account with you, as soon as any proper
thing can be thought on."[24] Presumably one thing that was "thought
on" was Johnson's "Life of Dr. Francis Cheynel," the first part of
which appeared in Vol. II, no. VII of Newbery's *The Student* (1751).

It would seem unusual, however, for Johnson to be turning to
Newbery for money if they had not had any previous business transactions. In fact, the letters indicate both by their brevity and confi-
dent tone that such a relationship had been established. Surely it is
possible — as suggested above — that Newbery may have been the
financial backer of John Payne in publishing the *Rambler*, and through
Payne Johnson may have first met Newbery.

In addition to the *Rambler*, Payne was associated with Johnson in
several other works during this period: *A New Prologue . . . at the
Presentation of Comus . . .* (1750) and Lauder's *Essay on Milton's
Use and Imitation of the Moderns . . .* (1750) were both published by
John Payne and his partner J. Bouquet. All the original folio numbers of the *Rambler* list the names of both partners on the imprint.
But Payne apparently bought out Bouquet sometime between March
and July, 1752, because the fifth and sixth volumes of the first duo-
decimo edition of the *Rambler*, which were published on July 27,
1752,[25] carry only Payne's name on the imprint. This is also true of
the reissue of all six volumes in the same year. Later, when
Hawkesworth, Johnson, Warton, and others were contributing to the
Adventurer in 1753—54, the only name on the imprint was that of
J. Payne. He was also the sole publisher of Johnson's edition of Sir
Thomas Browne's *Christian Morals* in 1756.

There is no evidence to suggest that Newbery had any share in the
Adventurer, but he certainly inaugurated the *Universal Chronicle* in
1758, and Payne was the publisher of at least the first thirty-nine
issues (i.e., all of Volume I).[26] Newbery apparently remained in
control throughout the life of the periodical, even though the publishers changed. As W. J. Bate says, ". . . the frequency and apparent
ease in the shift of publishers may suggest that there was some continuity behind the scenes to direct or absorb the changes."[27]

On May 19, 1759 Johnson borrowed £42/19/10 from Newbery,
and on March 20, 1760 he borrowed an additional £30.[28] During
this period Johnson was writing not only for the *Universal Chronicle*
but also for Newbery's new periodical, the *Public Ledger*.[29] Johnson
also contributed to Newbery's *World Displayed* in the fall of 1759.[30]

Furthermore, he wrote prefaces and dedications to works which
members of the "syndicate" were publishing. One good example of
Johnson's writing for Newbery may be found in the Rev. John

Lindsay's *Evangelical History of our Lord Jesus Christ* . . . (London: J. Newbery . . . and B. Collins in Salisbury, 1757). In 1761 Lindsay wrote a letter in which he refers to the book and admits that it "was indeed compiled by me alone; but the bookseller, (at whose request I wrote it,) had a mind to make a *society*, by desiring Mr. Johnson, the Dictionarian, to adorn it with a Dedication, to persons with whom I never had the honour of any correspondence" (Hazen, p. 117). Hazen continues by saying that the letter establishes some facts: namely, ". . . that the compilation was one of Newbery's projects, and that the dedication was solicited by Newbery. Both facts fit well with what is known of Newbery's activities at that period."

In the light of these facts, it is no surprise to learn that the majority of works for which Johnson wrote prefaces or dedications during the years 1756–63 were published by members of the "syndicate."[31] But one must not overstate the case. Surely it is probable that Johnson may have contributed to some of these works because the authors of them were his friends. Nevertheless, the high incidence of the names of the "syndicate" members on this list cannot be accidental, especially if one remembers that they were not the publishers with whom Johnson normally did business. With the exception of Dodsley – and he cannot rightfully be considered a member of the group – Johnson seems to have been careful to keep separate the publishers of his "literary" works and the publishers of his periodical essays and journalistic writings. It is surely significant that even during the period when Johnson was closely associated with the "syndicate," not one of its members has his name included in the imprint of the *Dictionary, Rasselas*, or the edition of Shakespeare. Nor can this selective choice of publishers be explained by entertaining the idea that the members of the "syndicate" were loath to publish literary, non-journalistic writings; far from it. Aside from Johnson, the three major authors who wrote for the "syndicate" – Christopher Smart, Oliver Goldsmith, and Tobias Smollett – all had some of their major literary works published by a member of the "syndicate," usually by John Newbery or his associates B. Collins or T. Carnan. Johnson did not, and this apparent selectivity in choosing publishers may be explained in several ways. It may be mere chance – that is, a chance beginning of business transactions with certain men may have become customary. It may possibly involve Johnson's sense of taste or propriety – that is, he deliberately chose to do hack work only for certain publishers. Whatever the reasons, there is no doubt that he would do every type of writing – even advertisements – for money, but his more "literary" writings were published by such men as Dodsley, Strahan, Millar, Cadell, and Nichols. Newbery and his "syndicate" were not included.[32]

II. The Nature and Duration of Johnson's Association
with the *Literary Magazine*

It is probable that at some time late in 1755 John Newbery and
other members of the "syndicate"[33] arranged to start a new monthly
magazine, to be staffed by William Faden, Samuel Johnson, probably
Griffith Jones, and perhaps others. As mentioned above, Faden
apparently served initially in the triple capacity of main editor,
printer, and publisher; Jones was apparently a contributor, and as
a member of the syndicate may have had some editorial responsibility
as well, at least until July, 1757, when he may have become editor of
the *London Chronicle*.[34]

The precise nature of Johnson's duties with the magazine is
uncertain. Arthur Murphy merely says that in 1756 Johnson "became
a reviewer in the Literary Magazine."[35] Sir John Hawkins in his *Life*
says that Johnson "assumed or submitted to the office of a reviewer,
as it is called, for the publisher of a monthly collection, entitled,
'The Literary Magazine.' "[36] Boswell states that Johnson "engaged
also to superintend and contribute largely to" the *Literary Magazine*.[37]

There are several things to support the theory that Johnson may
have been more than a book reviewer. First is the obvious fact that
he contributed a great deal more to the magazine than book reviews.[38]
Aside from the reviews of books (listed below), the items which
I believe Johnson wrote are:

1. "To the PUBLIC." *LM*, I, no. I (May, 1756), *iii*–iv.

2. "An Introduction to the Political State of Great-Britain."
   LM, I, no. I (May, 1756), *1* 2–9.

3. The Remarks in the "EXTRACT of the bill for the better
   ordering the Militia Forces in the several counties of that part
   of GREAT-BRITAIN called ENGLAND, as altered and
   amended by the committee, with REMARKS." *LM*, I, no. II
   (May 15 – June 15, 1756), *57* 58–63.

4. "OBSERVATIONS on the foregoing LETTER" [i.e., "A Letter
   from a French Refugee in America . . ."]. *LM*, I, no. II (May
   15 – June 15, 1756), 66–67.

5. "Observations on the foregoing Treaties" [i.e., ". . . a Treaty
   between His Britannic Majesty and her Imperial Majesty of all
   the Russias . . . December 11, 1742" and ". . . a Treaty between
   His Britannic Majesty and the Landgrave of Hesse-Cassel . . .
   June 18, 1755"]. *LM*, I, no. III (June 15 – July 15, 1756),
   119–121.

6.   "OBSERVATIONS on the present State of Affairs." *LM*, I,
      no. IV (July 15 — August 15, 1756), *161* 162—165.

7.   It is probable that Johnson wrote parts of the "Historical
      Memoirs" in the first four issues of the *Literary Magazine*; see
      Greene, items 18, 42, 67 and 88.

8.   "Memoirs of the King of Prussia," *LM*, I, no. VII (October 15 —
      November 15, 1756), *327* 328—333; "The Life of the King of
      Prussia continued," *LM*, I, no. VIII (November 15 — December
      15, 1756), *383* 384—390; "Life of the King of Prussia . . .
      concluded," *LM*, I, no. IX (December 15 [1756] — January 15,
      1757), *439* 440—442.

Listed here are original contributions only; I omit reprints of items
such as the proposals for Johnson's edition of Shakespeare and some
"Idler" papers.

The second bit of evidence is found in a letter which he wrote to
Robert Chambers dated 31 July 1756:

> Your Life came indeed too late for the month, but we
> suffered no inconvenience from the delay, because we had
> more materials than room. I have sent it already to the press,
> unread, for the next month, and am much obliged to you for
> doing it. I will contrive to find you more work. If you could
> send us any performances from Oxford they would be of
> great advantage to us. I wish you could add something to
> the printed accounts of any events that happen among you.
> I shall take care to send you the monthly month [mistake for
> "number" or "issue"?] gratis, if you contribute to it. But
> you must not tell that I have any thing in it. For though it is
> known conjecturally I would not have it made certain.[39]

Johnson is surely talking and acting like an editor here.

The third piece of evidence concerns possible reasons for the delay
in starting the magazine. The first number was to be that for January,
1756, and the newspapers advertised that the January number was to
be published on February 2, 1756.[40] The first issue, however, was
not published until May 15.[41] One possible reason for the delay was
Johnson's illness during late 1755 and early 1756. His poor state of
health is indicated by extracts from his letters:

> Dec. 29, 1755: I have never been out of doors since you saw
> me . . . I had then a cough so violent that I once fainted under
> its convulsions . . . My Physician bled me yesterday and the
> day before . . .

> Dec. 30, 1755: There has gone about a report that I died
> to day which I mention, lest you should hear it and be
> alarmed.
> [Mar.] 19, 1756: The inflammation is come again into
> my eye, so that I can read very little.
> April 15, 1756: For my part, I have not lately done much.
> I have been ill in the winter, and my eye has been inflamed,
> but I please myself with the hopes of doing many things
> with which I have long pleased and deceived myself.[42]

If Johnson had been assigned a major part in undertaking the new
magazine, his sickness might very well account for the delay in
publication. His return to health in mid-April would have allowed
him a month to prepare copy for the first issue.

Finally, it seems to have been customary for authors (and author-
editors) to enter into contractual agreements with the proprietors of
periodical publications. For example, on January 20, 1745/46, Mark
Akenside signed an agreement with Robert Dodsley to edit and to
contribute to *The Museum*.[43] On November 11, 1755 Christopher
Smart and Richard Rolt signed a contract with Edmund Allen, the
printer, and Thomas Gardner, the publisher, to edit and to contribute
to the *Universal Visiter*.[44] Goldsmith told Percy that in 1757 he had
an "agreem^t (which was in writing)" with Griffiths to write for the
Monthly Review for "board, Lodging, & 100^{ll} per annum" (*Collected
Works*, I, 3). According to Prior, Goldsmith also had a written financial agreement with Newbery for supplying his *Citizen of the World*
essays to the *Public Ledger*.[45] It seems probable that Johnson had
an agreement with Newbery not only to contribute to the *Universal
Chronicle* but also "to share directly in the profit."[46]

On the basis of these few examples it would be rash to make any
generalizations about author-publisher contracts in the mid-eighteenth
century, and it is clearly impossible to say much about the details of
Johnson's business relationships with Newbery. The most one can say
is that Johnson quite possibly had some form of written agreement
with Newbery, Faden, and perhaps others and that it may have
involved editorial obligations as well as contributions as an author.
Since Johnson was well known after the publication of the *Rambler*
and the *Dictionary*, his contract — if he had one — may also have
called for a share of the profits. Indeed, if Hawkins is correct in
stating that Johnson shared in the profits of Newbery's *Universal
Chronicle*, it is not unlikely that he may have done so with the
Literary Magazine.

Regardless of the precise nature of Johnson's agreement with the
managers of the *Literary Magazine*, it is certain that he did not remain

associated with it throughout its entire run of twenty-seven issues. But when he left the magazine, and why, are questions not easy to answer.

On March 8, 1758 Johnson wrote to his friend Charles Burney, saying, in part, "Since the Life of Brown I have been a little engaged, from time to time in the *Literary Magazine*, but not very lately."[47] Unfortunately, the letter gives no further clue as to how much earlier than March 8 he may have ceased to be engaged in the magazine. Arthur Murphy relates the following in his *Essay* on Johnson:

> Mr. Nichols, whose attachment to his illustrious friend was unwearied, shewed him [Johnson] in 1780 a book, called *Remarks on Johnson's Life of Milton*, in which the affair of Lauder was renewed with virulence, and a *poetical scale* in the Literary Magazine 1758 (when Johnson had ceased to write in that collection) was urged as an additional proof of deliberate malice. He read the libellous passage with attention, and instantly wrote on the margin: ' "In the business of Lauder I was deceived, partly by thinking the man too frantic to be fraudulent." Of the *poetical scale* quoted from the Magazine I am not the author. I fancy it was put in after I had quitted that work; for I not only did not write it, but I do not remember it.'[48]

Since the "Poetical Scale" appeared in the January, 1758 issue of the *Literary Magazine* (pp. 6—8), we therefore have both Murphy and Johnson himself telling us that Johnson was not associated with the magazine in 1758 (i.e., all of Vol. III).

Johnson's last known contribution to the magazine was the final installment of his review of Soame Jenyns' *Free Inquiry*, which appeared in Vol. II, no. XV (1757), published on July 19, 1757.[49] Everyone who has ever discussed the duration of Johnson's connection with the magazine —beginning with the *European Magazine* in 1784—85 — has agreed that Johnson stopped with that issue. No one has ever advanced any arguments for an earlier or later point of termination.

Greene argues (pp. 390—92) that political differences were the cause of Johnson's leaving the magazine:

> It is apparent at a glance that the *Literary Magazine*, in spite of its name, was throughout its career a political organ. Its politics at the outset were distinctly anti-Newcastle. It was known that Johnson was certainly no great lover of the Walpole-Newcastle Whig 'connexion', and the entrepreneur of the *Magazine* (whoever that may have been) might well have

had that thought in mind when inviting Johnson to 'superintend'
it.

. . . Johnson's political contributions to the *Magazine* manifest
a clear, consistent, and emphatic set of opinions: he is anti-
commercialist, anti-imperialist, anti-expansionist, in the
'old Tory' tradition, which was closer to Walpole and
Newcastle in these matters than it was to Pitt. . . .

By the spring of 1757, however, Newcastle and Pitt formed
a coalition ministry, so Johnson's criticism of the government,
which was appropriate while Pitt led the opposition, was no longer
needed. "At any rate," Greene continues, "whether it was through
the accidents of shifting political alliances, or through an actual
change in the ownership of the *Magazine* (which its variety of
imprints may well indicate), the periodical now became violently
patriotic, completely reversing the attitude toward the war that
had been expressed by Johnson."[50] Surely it is reasonable to believe
that if Johnson and the managers of the magazine differed forcefully
in their political opinions, the managers would not allow him to
contribute further political essays. However, although it is correct
that Johnson did not contribute specifically political essays beyond
the fourth issue of the magazine, he did continue to express the
same political opinions in some of his book reviews (especially those
of Lewis Evans and the Byng pamphlets) in issues no. 6, 7, 9 and 12.
Furthermore, the same "syndicate" hired Johnson again in 1758 to
write for the *Universal Chronicle*, where once more he stated his
opinions on politics and the conduct of the war (as well as many other
topics). I doubt, therefore, whether political differences alone were
strong enough to cause Johnson to leave the magazine.

I believe that there were three additional reasons, all related,
which caused Johnson finally to leave the magazine. The first is
purely financial: the magazine was not successful with the public.
On July 30, 1756 Johnson wrote a long letter to Mrs. Charlotte
Lennox in which he gives her some advice on literary matters. He
then discusses her translation of the *Memoirs of . . . the Duke of
Sully*, and offers his assistance in trying to get the book reviewed:

> If you can point me out a passage [in *Sully*] that can be
> refered to the present times, I will press for a place in the
> Gentleman's Magazine, and write an Introduction to it,
> if I can not get it in there I will put it in the new book
> [the *Literary Magazine*], but their readers are, I think,
> seven to one.[51]

Johnson's efforts with the former were apparently unsuccessful, for

a few months later he reviewed the book in the *Literary Magazine*.[52]
The significant point here, however, is Johnson's account of the
circulation statistics of the two magazines. I have been unable to
find any circulation figures for the *Gentleman's Magazine* in 1756;
but ten years earlier Cave refers with delight to "an increased and
unexpected demand of 3,000 Magazines monthly."[53] If in the
ensuing decade the *Gentleman's Magazine* increased its circulation
by one-third or even one-half, a ratio of seven to one still would
indicate that the *Literary Magazine* had pitifully few readers.

If we assume that Johnson had a profit-sharing contract with the
"syndicate," it probably contained an escape clause similar to the
one in the contract of the *Universal Visiter*: if profits were too low,
then all contracts were cancelled. The *Literary Magazine* apparently
never gained great circulation; and after working on it for more than
a year, Johnson may have exercised a contractual option and left.
Even if he had no contract, he may have decided not to work for
an unprofitable magazine any longer.

The "syndicate" did not let one of its publications fail without
making valiant efforts to try to save it. As we have seen, several of
the same men started the *London Chronicle* in January, 1757, and
it was instantly successful. The newspaper, therefore, was used in
various ways to try to stimulate the lagging circulation of the
magazine.[54] Another thing the "syndicate" did was to allow
several of its members to take turns being publisher (and main
editor?) of the magazine to see what they could do for it. As was
mentioned above, Faden published the first nine issues; J. Richardson
the next ten; and finally, late in 1757, John Wilkie, the successful
publisher of the *London Chronicle*, assumed control of the magazine
for what proved to be its final eight issues.[55] I believe that the pros-
pect of Wilkie's becoming publisher may have been an important
factor in Johnson's leaving the magazine.

Johnson's review of the second edition of Hanway's *Journal of
Eight Days Journey* appeared in the thirteenth issue of the *Literary
Magazine*, which was published on May 17, 1757.[56] Surely by no
coincidence, the *London Chronicle* of the same day contains a short
notice with a quotation from Hanway and Johnson's comment upon
it.[57]

> Mr. H. in his Essay on Tea, addressed to some Ladies, tells
> them, 'That though Tea and Gin have spread their baleful
> Influence over this Island, and his Majesty's other Dominions,
> yet they might be assured that the Governors of the Foundling-
> Hospital would exert their utmost Skill and Vigilance to
> prevent the Children under their Care from being poisoned, or

enervated by one or the other.' Upon which Passage
a truly good Man, and very able Writer, makes the
following Remark in the Literary Magazine: 'I know
not upon what Observation Mr. Hanway founds his
Confidence in the Governors of the Foundling-Hospital,
Men of whom I have not any Knowledge, but whom
I intreat to consider a little the Minds, as well as Bodies
of the Children. I am inclined to believe Irreligion equally
pernicious with Gin and Tea, and therefore think it not
unseasonable to mention, that when, a few Months ago,
I wandered through the Hospital, I found not a Child
that seemed to have heard of his Creed, or the Command-
ments. To breed up Children in this Manner, is to rescue
them from an early Grave, that they may find Employment for the Gibbet; from dying in Innocence, that they
may perish by their Crimes.'

The account of the events following the publication of this brief
article is well presented by Ruth K. McClure in her excellent article,
"Johnson's Criticism of the Foundling Hospital and its Consequences."[58]
She shows the reasons why "the Governors' sensitivity to unfavourable
comment had been refined by years of courting public goodwill"
(McClure, p. 18). The *Gazetteer* of May 18 reprinted the article from
the *Chronicle* of the day before, and this further aroused the Governors.
At the meeting of the Foundling Hospital's General Committee on
May 25, 1757, the Hospital's solicitor, Mr. Plumptre, was directed
"to visit the printers of the *Literary Magazine* and the two newspapers
and to insist that they disclose who had written the review. If they
refused to do so, he was authorized to threaten them with prosecution
according to law" (McClure, p. 19). Jonas Hanway, however, did not
wait for the results of this investigation, and his response was printed
in the *Gazetteer* of May 26, 1757.[59] Not receiving satisfaction from
the periodicals involved, the Hospital's General Committee at their
weekly meeting on June 8 directed Mr. Plumptre to "give notice to
the Publishers of the said Magazine, and of the said Chronicle &
Gazetteer, that they will be prosecuted according to law for the
publication of the said Libel unless they severally make a proper
satisfaction to this Hospital" (quoted by McClure, p. 20). This threat
produced results, and representatives of the periodicals attended the
meeting of the Committee on June 15. John Wilkie, representing the
Chronicle, and Charles Say, the printer and manager of the *Gazetteer*,
told the Governors "that the paragraphs which reflected on this
Corporation were inserted in their papers without their knowledge,
and that they would insert a Paragraph in their Papers to acknowledge

A Paragraph having been copied from the Literary Magazine in this Paper of the 17th of May laft, reflecting on the Governors and Guardians of the Hofpital for the Maintenance and Education of expofed and deferted young Children, as if the Children of that Hofpital were not educated in the Principles of the Chriftian Religion; I think it a Piece of Juftice due to thofe Gentlemen, who generoufly take upon themfelves the Direction and Management of fo noble and excellent a Charity, to declare, that, upon Enquiry, I find what is there contained is entirely groundlefs——The Children of that Hofpital are obliged not only to attend the Service of the Church twice every Sunday in the Chapel, but are catechized alfo every Sunday in the Afternoon publickly in the Summer, and privately in the Winter; they are likewife privately inftructed by a proper Mafter and Miftreffes, in Reading the Scriptures, and in the Principles of the Chriftian Religion; and obliged to fay their Prayers Morning and Evening, according to a Form prepared for them by one of the greateft Divines of the Church of England, and approved by the Governors: I do, therefore, hereby afk Pardon of the faid Governors for publifhing fo falfe and injurious an Afperfion.   J. Wilkie.

II.   John Wilkie's apology in the *London Chronicle* of June 16—18, 1757

the offence" (quoted by McClure, pp. 20–21). Wilkie's retraction was printed in the *London Chronicle* of June 18 (i.e., dated June 16–18, 1757):

A Paragraph having been copied from the Literary Magazine in this Paper of the 17th of May last, reflecting on the Governors and Guardians of the Hospital for the Maintenance and Education of exposed and deserted young Children, as if the Children of that Hospital were not educated in the Principles of the Christian Religion; I think it a Piece of Justice due to those Gentlemen, who generously take upon themselves the Direction and Management of so noble and excellent a Charity, to declare, that, upon Enquiry, I find what is there contained is entirely groundless – The Children of that Hospital are obliged not only to attend the Service of the Church twice every Sunday in the Chapel, but are catechized also every Sunday in the Afternoon publickly in the Summer, and privately in the Winter; they are likewise privately instructed by a proper Master and Mistresses, in Reading the Scriptures, and in the Principles of the Christian Religion; and obliged to say their Prayers Morning and Evening, according to a Form prepared for them by one of the greatest Divines of the Church of England, and approved by the Governors; I do, therefore, hereby ask Pardon of the said Governors for publishing so false and injurious an Aspersion.

J. Wilkie.

One wonders if at any other time in his life Johnson was ever so publicly branded a liar, especially in a published article signed by a member of the group for which he was working. To make matters worse, Johnson must have known that Wilkie was scheduled to assume control of the *Literary Magazine*. The very thought of having to work with and for such a man must have been intolerable.

J. Richardson, the current publisher of the *Literary Magazine*, was also present at the meeting on June 15 but proved less cooperative than Wilkie or Say. He "denied that it was in his power to discover [i.e., reveal] the Author" and added "that the Author would avow the truth of the said Libel" (McClure, p. 21). He knew, of course, that Johnson's reply was already at press; it was printed in the fourteenth issue of the *Literary Magazine* (*LM*, II, 253–56 [misnumbered 356]), which was published June 17, 1757, the day before Wilkie published his retraction. Johnson's reply was, says Boswell, "the only instance, I believe, in the whole course of his life, when he condescended to oppose anything that was written against him . . . .

But, indeed, the good Mr. Hanway laid himself so open to ridicule, that Johnson's animadversions upon his attack were chiefly to make sport."[60] Johnson probably considered the threat of a libel suit ample reason to depart from precedent by replying to an attacker. Although ostensibly merely answering Hanway's piece in the *Gazetteer* of May 26, Johnson's reply constitutes a thorough justification and defense of his previous statements. One of the most effective pieces of prose that ever came from Johnson's pen, it is witty and forceful enough to demolish anything written by a Hanway or a Wilkie. Johnson's reply also provides the basis for the defense in a civil action (tort) for libel: he was stating the truth (and could prove it by his witnesses), and the necessary element of malice was absent. Johnson answered Hanway to defend Richardson, his publisher, who had consistently refused to divulge the name of the author. In view of this refusal, the Governors ordered "that the Sollicitor of this Corporation do attend the Attorney General, and take his advice in the carrying on a Prosecution against the said Mr. Richardson, and do follow his Instructions in carrying on such Prosecution" (quoted by McClure, p. 22). Ruth McClure argues (pp. 22–24) that the Governors probably planned to bring a criminal suit for libel, in which the truth of the defamatory words was irrelevant. "But the Attorney General must have advised against such an action, for no prosecution was commenced, and no mention of the affair ever appeared again in the Hospital's records" (McClure, p. 23).

The Hospital does not seem to have suffered in any way from this incident, but we are free to speculate about several other results. As was discussed above, Charles Spens had been the editor of the *London Chronicle* since it was initiated on January 1, 1757; but when James Emonson began a new paper entitled *Lloyd's Evening Post* in July, 1757, Spens was its editor. He had survived the storm in January over the *Test* and *Con-Test*, at which time Robert Dodsley had quit the partnership. But surely the members of the "syndicate" held him responsible for material printed in the newspaper; so after Wilkie as publisher had to sustain the threat of an action for libel, he and other members probably decided to ease Spens out. The timing of Spens's new job with Emonson would tend to corroborate this speculation.

Did the same people react in the same way to this libel incident by removing Johnson from the staff of the *Literary Magazine*? There is no evidence for this, but I suspect there was a mutual willingness to part company. Johnson had contributed very little to the magazine in the spring of 1757, and the libel incident probably led the members of the "syndicate" to believe that Johnson's departure would not be a great loss to the magazine. Johnson also had his reasons for being

discouraged and restless. Since the fall of 1756 he had been
increasingly at odds with the political position taken by the magazine.
Financially, even if he had a profit-sharing contract, he was probably
receiving very little money from it. The circulation of the magazine
was discouragingly small, and it must have hurt his professional pride
to be furnishing well-written material to a periodical which few people
ever saw. As he looked to the future, it must have been extremely
distasteful to think of working for John Wilkie. Moreover, Johnson's
edition of Shakespeare was beckoning. So he helped to defend his
publisher Richardson — and his own reputation for truth and
accuracy — by contributing his final, forceful essay against Hanway;
and after it was published in the fourteenth issue of the *Literary
Magazine* on June 17, 1757, Johnson wrote for the magazine no
more.[61]

III. The Canon of Johnson's Book Reviews
in the *Literary Magazine*

On March 8, 1758 Johnson wrote a letter to his friend Charles
Burney in which he mentions the *Literary Magazine* and says, "I have
not the collection by me, and therefore cannot draw out a catalogue
of my own parts, but will do it, and send it. Do not buy them, for
I will gather all those that have any thing of mine in them, and send
them to Mrs. Burney, as a small token of gratitude for the regard
which she is pleased to bestow upon me."[62] The discovery of such
a list (or group of clippings) — assuming that it was ever compiled —
is the only sure way of determining accurately Johnson's contributions to the magazine. However, the "catalogue" is not now among
the extant Burney manuscripts.[63]
Since Johnson's own documents are not available, all investigators
of his canon have been forced to rely on what Johnson said (or
reports of what he said) plus their evaluation of evidence, both
internal and external. The complex and often haphazard way in which
the canon of Johnson's contributions to the *Literary Magazine* has
developed has been discussed in an admirable fashion by Donald J.
Greene.[64] He is undoubtedly correct in emphasizing the fact that
there is nothing sacrosanct in Boswell's list. Yet, he continues,

> There is this much reason for assurance, however: none of
> the skilled Johnsonians who may be presumed to have examined
> all the pieces attributed in the list — among others, Malone,
> Alexander Chalmers, Croker, Hill, Powell, Hazen —has been

seriously enough disturbed by any of them to raise a doubt
that it is by Johnson . . . .
    I am inclined to take a liberal position, generally, regarding
Johnson's part in the early numbers, at least, of the magazine:
I am willing, along with other students from Malone to
Hazen, to accept the Boswell-Courtney attributions.[65]

I too accept these attributions. Therefore the first group of items
I present here are those of Boswell and Courtney, listed in the order
in which they appear in the *Literary Magazine,* and numbered and
titled according to the list at the beginning of Chapter II, below.
I adopt Greene's policy of presenting the original source of the
attribution in parentheses after each item. A detailed description
of each book reviewed, including a transcription of every title-page,
is also given in Chapter II.

The Twenty-seven Reviews listed by Boswell and Courtney

    See Chapter II, below.

1. [Ch. II, no. 3] Thomas Birch, *The History of the Royal Society,*
     Vol. I–II. (1791 Boswell *Life*)
2. [Ch. II, no. 4] Arthur Murphy, *The Gray's-Inn Journal,* Vol.
     I–II. (1791 Boswell *Life*)
3. [Ch. II, no. 5] Joseph Warton, *Essay on Pope,* Vol. I. (1789
     George Gleig *Works* Vol. XV)
4. [Ch. II, no. 6] James Hampton (trans.), *History of Polybius*
     (1791 Boswell *Life*)
5. [Ch. II, no. 7] Thomas Blackwell, *Memoirs of the Court of
     Augustus* (1774 Davies, *Miscellaneous and
     Fugitive Pieces,* Vol. III; 1774 *Gentleman's
     Magazine* Nov., p. 525; 1787 Hawkins *Life,*
     p. 351 and *Works,* Vol. X)
6. [Ch. II, no. 8] Alexander Russell, *The Natural History of
     Aleppo* (1789 George Gleig *Works,* Vol. XV)
7. [Ch. II, no. 9] Sir Isaac Newton, *Four Letters to Bentley*
     (1773 Davies, *Miscellaneous and Fugitive
     Pieces,* Vol. I; 1774 *Gentleman's Magazine*
     Nov., p. 524; 1787 *Works,* Vol. X)
8. [Ch. II, no. 10] William Borlase, *Observations on the Islands of
     Scilly* (1791 Boswell *Life*)
9. [Ch. II, no. 13] Francis Home, *Experiments on Bleaching* (1791
     Boswell *Life*)

10. [Ch. II, no. 14] Sir Thomas Browne, *Christian Morals*, 2d ed. (1791 Boswell *Life*)
11. [Ch. II, no. 15] Stephen Hales, *An Account of a Useful Discovery* (1791 Boswell *Life* — though not listed in Greene, "Development," p. 417)
12. [Ch. II, no. 16] Charles Lucas, *An Essay on Waters* (1789 George Gleig *Works* Vol. XV)
13. [Ch. II, no. 17] Robert Keith, *Catalogue of the Bishops of Scotland* (1791 Boswell *Life*)
14. [Ch. II, no. 18] Patrick Browne, *Civil and Natural History of Jamaica* (1791 Boswell *Life*)
15. [Ch. II, no. 20] *Philosophical Transactions*, Vol. XLIX, Pt. I, for 1755 (1791 Boswell *Life*)
16. [Ch. II, no. 22] Mrs. Charlotte Lennox (trans.), *Memoirs of the Duke of Sully* (1789 George Gleig *Works*, Vol. XV)
17. [Ch. II, no. 23] Elizabeth Harrison, *Miscellanies* (1789 George Gleig *Works* Vol. XV -- though not listed in Greene, "Development," p. 417)
18. [Ch. II, no. 24] Lewis Evans, *Geographical . . . Essays . . . the First* (1789 George Gleig *Works* Vol. XV)
19. [Ch. II, no. 25] *A Letter to a Member of Parliament . . . Relative to the Case of Admiral Byng* (1788 *Works* Supp. Vol. XIV)
20. [Ch. II, no. 26] John Shebbeare, *An Appeal to the People . . . Part I* (1788 *Works* Supp. Vol. XIV)
21. [Ch. II, no. 27] Jonas Hanway, *A Journal of Eight Days Journey . . .* 1st ed., 4° (1787 Hawkins *Life*, 1st ed., p. 355)
22. [Ch. II, no. 28] Samuel Bever, *The Cadet* (1791 Boswell *Life*)
23. [Ch. II, no. 29] *Some further Particulars* [re. Byng] (1791 Boswell *Life*)
24. [Ch. II, no. 30] David Mallet, *The Conduct of the Ministry Impartially Examined* (1788 *Works* Supp. Vol. XIV)
25. [Ch. II, no. 37] Jonas Hanway, *A Journal of Eight Days Journey . . .* 2d ed., 2 vols., 8° (1787 Hawkins *Life*, 1st ed., p. 355)
26. [Ch. II, no. 38] Soame Jenyns, *A Free Inquiry into the Nature and Origin of Evil* (1773 Davies, *Miscellaneous and Fugitive Pieces*, Vol. I; 1774 *Gentleman's Magazine* Nov., p. 524; 1787 Hawkins *Life*)
27. [Ch. II, no. 39] Jonas Hanway, A Paper in the *Gazetteer* of May 26, 1757 (1785 *European Magazine* Feb., p. 83)

Each of the twenty-seven items listed here is included in the lists of
Boswell, Courtney, Bloom and the *CBEL*, although Boswell in his
list does not differentiate the two reviews of Hanway's *Journal of
Eight Days Journey* . . . .[66]

Thus, of the twenty-seven items, twelve were attributed by
Boswell in his *Life* and six by George Gleig in Vol. XV of the *Works*,
published in 1789. In his "General Preface" Gleig says that "the
several reviews, with the dedication of *the Evangelical History
harmonized*, are ascribed to him by a lady to whom he was long
known, whose mind he successfully cultivated, and whose name,
were it mentioned, would remove every suspicion. Indeed the author
of these elegant tracts cannot be mistaken . . ." (p. 7). The lady has
been proved correct in attributing to Johnson the dedication of the
Evangelical History (see Hazen, p. 117). Greene suggests (p. 369)
that the lady may have been Mrs. Charlotte Lennox, and he is
probably right. The recently discovered letter of Johnson to
Mrs. Lennox dated July 30, 1756 (see above) serves to confirm the
attribution to Johnson of the review of Mrs. Lennox' translation of
Sully's *Memoirs*, and surely it strengthens the possibility that
Mrs. Lennox was the informant of George Gleig.

In Chapter II, below, a total of thirty-nine reviews are listed as
Johnson's. As we have just seen, Boswell and Courtney list twenty-
seven; of the remaining twelve, six have been attributed to Johnson
at some time since 1940 and six others are here attributed to him for
the first time. In each case the review is listed and then the attribution
is discussed.

[Ch. II, no. 19]   Charles Parkin, *Account of the Invasion under
                    William Duke of Normandy*
Donald J. Greene believes that he is the first to attribute this
review to Johnson,[67] but it was initially ascribed to Johnson by
D. Nichol Smith (*CBEL*, II, 620). I accept the attribution.

[Ch. II, no. 21]   John George Keysler, *Travels through Germany* . . .
                    Vol. I
In 1955 Arthur Sherbo attributed this review to Johnson,[68] and
the following year Donald J. Greene concurred without comment.[69]
I accept the attribution because I agree with most of Sherbo's arguments. But I have doubts about a few: Sherbo lists several extracts
from Keysler which the reviewer in the *Literary Magazine* made; and
since the subjects of these extracts coincide with Johnson's known
interests, Sherbo suggests that the reviewer was Johnson. This may
be so, but some of the same extracts appealed to other critics who
wrote reviews in other periodicals before the review in the *Literary*

Magazine was published. Gregory Sharpe wrote the review in the
Monthly Review[70] and Thomas Francklin that in the *Critical
Review*.[71] Both start with short accounts of Keysler's life; the
Critical Review quotes the description of the University of Tubingen;
and the *Monthly Review* quotes the account of Patkul and Charles
XII. Such points of agreement with the review in the *Literary Magazine* may all be coincidence, and I am not suggesting that the writer
in the *Literary Magazine* borrowed from these reviews; but if the
attribution to Johnson is based on the choice of extracts, surely the
attribution is weakened somewhat by finding that other writers
chose some of the same extracts at an earlier date.

[Ch. II, no. 1]   John Armstrong, *The History of the Island of
                   Minorca*
    Greene argues for this review (pp. 374–77) in one of his most
convincing attributions. I agree completely, although I must make
two modifications in Greene's statements. He states, without presenting
evidence, that the article is based on the first edition of Armstrong's
History (London, 1752). Surely Johnson reviewed an issue published
in April, 1756. Of the four issues of the book, I argue (see Chapter
II, item no. 1) that Johnson reviewed the third, which I label issue C.
It also contains the "Letter from an Officer at Minorca," dated
February 27, 1756, which is reprinted verbatim in the *Literary Magazine*, I, no. I, 9–10. Greene does not know that the "Letter" is part
of Armstrong's *History*, and so he does not include it in the review.
I list it as an integral part of the review.

[Ch. II, no. 2]   Stephen White, *Collateral Bee-Boxes*
    Greene argues (pp. 377–78) that this review is by Johnson, and
I agree, although the attribution is based on little evidence. Greene
believes that the review is an example of dry, Johnsonian humor, and
he is probably right. I believe that the condensations are made in such
a masterful way that they almost bear the trademark of Samuel
Johnson. They are quite distinctive, and I have not found another
reviewer of the period who could equal his skill (see Chapter III,
below).

[Ch. II, no. 11]   John Douglas, *Six Letters from A——d B——r*

[Ch. II, no. 12]   Archibald Bower, *Affidavit*
    The double review of these two pamphlets constitutes, without
a doubt, Greene's strongest and most convincing attribution
(pp. 381–83). He is, however, justifiably confused about the number
and titles of the pamphlets being reviewed. Both of the pamphlets
quote extensively from earlier writings, and later pamphlets quote

from them. The only way to solve the confusion was to examine and read the pamphlets involved, and to determine their dates of publication (see Appendix B). Thus we find that Douglas' *Six Letters* was published on June 28, 1756; that Bower's *Affidavit* appeared July 1, 1756; and that Johnson reviewed both of them in the third issue of the *Literary Magazine*, which was published on July 15, 1756.

Greene makes a more serious error in the last sentence of his account: "A continuation of the report on the Bower controversy is given in No. 9 of the *Magazine*, pp. 442–53, but this consists only of quotations without editorial comment" (p. 383). In fact, the "continuation" contains much editorial comment, which should be attributed to Samuel Johnson for the same strong reasons that Greene gives for the two earlier pieces. The continuation reviews two pamphlets:

[Ch. II, no. 31]   John Douglas, *Bower and Tillemont compared . . .*

[Ch. II, no. 32]   Archibald Bower, *Answer to a scurrilous Pamphlet . . .*

Douglas' pamphlet was published on January 6, 1757; Bower's pamphlet appeared the same day; and Johnson reviewed both of them in the ninth issue of the *Literary Magazine* which was published on January 20, 1757.

The review begins (pp. 442–49) with a long extract entitled "Mr. Bower's Account of the Inquisition at Macerata, and of his escape from Italy. (Taken from his own Mouth.)" This comprises a whole section of Douglas' *Bower and Tillemont compared . . . .* Johnson then says:

> This is the account given by the antagonist of Mr. *Bower*, as taken from Mr. *Bower*'s own mouth. Mr. *Bower* has at last published an account of his escape, in an *Answer to a scurrilous Pamphlet, &c.* The narrative which he has printed is conformable enough, in the first part, to that which he is said to have given in conversation, the slight disagreements between them being, as Mr. *Bower* himself allows, only failures of memory, and geographical mistakes.
>
> In the foregoing narrative the rewards offered by the inquisition are 300 £. for his person alive, and 600 £. for his head; in Mr. *Bower*'s, more probably, 800 crowns for his person, and 600 crowns for his head. In his own account there is no mention of his design to *travel on horseback through the Adriatic.* He tells nothing of the alarm spread through the canton of *Bern.*
>
> The chief variation between the two relations begins where Mr. *Bower* quitted the boat at *Strasburgh*, the account which

we have inserted having more omissions, and insertions,
than could easily have happened by chance or forgetfulness.
We shall therefore insert his own words.[72]

An extract from Bower then follows (pp. 449—50), after which
Johnson continues: "After the relation of his escape, Mr. *Bower*
proceeds to deliver the series of his life from his arrival in *England*,
of which we can only give a very contracted epitome." The *Magazine*
then presents in less than one column a brilliant condensation of
pages 30—41 of Bower's pamphlet. The whole passage is a fine example
of Johnson's skill. He then says: "Having thus given the general history
of his life. [sic] Mr. *Bower* proceeds to examine the particular facts
alledged against him" (p. 451). Johnson then condenses pages 41—79
of Bower's pamphlet into the space of two and a half columns, and
then continues:

> He now comes to the six letters of which he still denies
> the authenticity, and promises in his next pamphlet to
> detect them of forgery; he then spends a few pages in
> denying some of the stories told of his connections with
> papists, or levity of behaviour. At a house in *Covent-
> Garden* he owns he was once seen, but declares he entered
> it only to bring out a young man, and reconcile him to his
> father [p. 452].

There follows a condensation of pages 99—112 of Bower into one and
a half columns; then Johnson concludes:

> This is the long expected defence of Mr. *Bower* which I
> have endeavoured not to weaken by contracting it. He has
> defended himself not unskilfully if he be innocent; if he
> be guilty he has pleaded his cause with great ability. The
> proofs of the spuriousness of the letters are yet to come,
> and of them I shall only observe that proofs must be very
> strong that will counterbalance similitude of hand. To write
> a name so as to deceive is easy, to write a line is possible;
> to write a letter, and even six letters, in an imitated hand
> with success, I believe no man will undertake: Similitude
> of hand, if there be a sufficient quantity of writing to be
> compared, is a physical testimony, perhaps irrefragably
> cogent.
>   In the defence which we have just perused Mr. *Bower*
> allows that Father *Carteret* declared that *he had reconciled
> him to the Church*, and seems to endeavour to evade that
> assertion by fixing it on his adversary's mistaken opinion,
> that he was reconciled to the order.

While I was engaged in the foregoing extract Mr. *Faden*
has again declared to me that Mr. *Bower* converted Mrs.
Hoyles to popery; that in the years 1734 and 35, during
which Mr. *Faden* lodged in her house, Mr. *Bower* frequently
visited her, and was received and considered as a papist.

Here is an accusation confirmed by every kind of
evidence. It is known that Mrs. *Hoyles* and her husband
were converted to popery; it is known that about that
time Mr. *Bower* frequently visited her, and her conversion
is here imputed to him, and imputed to him by a Protestant
[p. 453].

I have absolutely no hesitation in attributing the review of these
two pamphlets to Johnson. The style sounds like Johnson, especially
in such passages as the first paragraph of the conclusion (quoted
above). His belief in the truthfulness of William Faden sounds
convincing and appropriate. (In his review of the first two Bower
pamphlets, Johnson quotes a passage and says that "This relation
is corroborated by the testimony of Mr. *Faden*, a man, whose
character will not suffer him to be considered as an exceptionable
witness."[73] Once again, his argument concerning "similitude of
hand" is very similar to the argument in his review of Tytler's
*Historical and Critical Enquiry into the Evidence . . . against Mary
Queen of Scots* (Edinburgh, 1760).[74] Greene's other argument is
also applicable here — namely, that this is another instance in which
Johnson is helping Douglas to unmask an impostor, just as he did
earlier in the Lauder-Milton controversy and as he did later in the
affair of the Cock-Lane ghost.[75]

The Bower pamphlet was also reviewed in three issues of the
London Chronicle, January 18—20, 20—22, and 22—25, 1757;
I believe its author was almost surely Arthur Murphy (see Preface,
above). He ends his article by quoting the conclusion of the review
in the *Literary Magazine*, which he introduces in these words: "The
masterly Writer who gives the Account of Books, printed in the
Literary Magazine, concludes his Extract . . . by observing . . . ."
He even introduces Johnson's final paragraph in this manner: "Here
is an Accusation (says the same candid and judicious Writer) confirmed by every kind of Evidence."[76] This type of flattery, and
indeed these very words, are typical of Murphy's references to
Johnson in the columns of the *London Chronicle* during this period
(see Preface and footnote 57, above). I believe it is additional evidence —
if any is needed — that Johnson is the reviewer in the *Literary Magazine*.

The review of the two Bower tracts is followed in the same issue of the *Magazine* by another double review. The items are:

[Ch. II, no. 33]   Arthur Murphy, Henry Fox, and others, *The Test*

[Ch. II, no. 34]   Owen Ruffhead, Philip Francis, and others, *The Con-Test*

William Pitt replaced Henry Fox as Secretary of State for the Southern Department on December 4, 1756, and the political rivalry between the two men was intense. Both before and after that date, this rivalry was expressed (in part) through pamphlets and periodicals. On November 6, 1756, the first of thirty-five numbers of *The Test* was published; and, losing no time, on November 23 the first of thirty-eight numbers of *The Con-Test* appeared.

I believe that Johnson reviewed these two political periodicals in January, 1757 to give moral support to Robert Dodsley in his argument with Charles Spens, editor of the *London Chronicle*. As we have seen, Dodsley insisted that the newspaper should not print invective and personal satire. In a letter to William Strahan dated January 14, 1757, Dodsley says: "There is another thing which I must mention, and that is, that we give no just cause of complaint to yᵉ Trade, either by taking the whole of any periodical Papers, or by giving such large extracts of Pamphlets as may prevent their sale, and consequently instead of serving injure the Proprietors. As to yᵉ *Tests*, *Contests* and all such Papers as deal in personal satire, we should certainly have nothing to do with them."[77] But Spens, of course, did not desist from printing personal attacks (including excerpts from the *Test* and *Con-Test*), and ten days later Dodsley withdrew as a partner from the *London Chronicle*. D. Nichol Smith suggests that the controversy over *The Test* and *The Con-Test* was the main reason for Dodsley's withdrawal.[78]

In view of this activity in the offices of the *London Chronicle*, it scarcely seems accidental that the reviewer in the *Literary Magazine* chose this time to review both of the political periodicals. The review appeared in the ninth issue of the magazine, which was published on January 20, 1757. The reviewer introduces his subject in this manner:

> *The Change of the Ministry has produced a Paper called the* TEST, *written in Favour of Mr. H. F. to defame Mr P. who is insulted with every invidious Recollection of the past, and anticipation of the future; the Charge which has been urged with most Humour and Spirit is, that since his Engagement in the Administration, he has not freed himself from the Gout. To this* Test *a zealous Writer has opposed a* CON-TEST. *Of both these Papers we shall exhibit Specimens.*[79]

Extensive extracts are then given from the first, second, and seventh issues of both periodicals. The reviewer then concludes:

> Of these papers of the *Test* and *Con-test* we have given a very copious specimen, and hope that we shall give no more. The debate seems merely personal, no one topic of general import having been yet attempted. Of the motives of the author of the *Test*, whoever he be, I believe, every man who speaks honestly, speaks with contempt. Of the *Con-Test*, which being defensive, is less blameable, I have yet heard no great commendation. The language is that of a man struggling after elegance and catching finery in its stead: the author of the *Con-test* is more knowing; of wit neither can boast, in the *Test* it is frequently attempted, but always by mean and despicable imitations, without the least glimmer of intrinsic light, without a single effort of original thought.[80]

The reviewer has contributed only these two paragraphs, but the style of both of them — especially the second — seems distinctively Johnsonian to me. Also, both the timing and the contents of the review suggest that it may have been written by a friend of Dodsley who agreed with him in his argument with Spens. Johnson's feelings towards Dodsley are well known, and it is appealing to think that Johnson tried to assist his old friend in this matter. I believe, despite the slender evidence available, that the review should be admitted to the canon.

[Ch. II, no. 35]   William Whitehead, *Elegies, with an Ode to the Tiber*

This review is so short that I give it in its entirety:

> We were highly pleased to see this work advertised; a muse returning from classic ground, naturally promised us an entertaining combination of poetic images, excited by a survey of the ruins of antient *Italy*, or the beautiful scenery which modern refinements have spread over the face of the country. Nor were we disappointed in this expectation. To speak first of the ode to the *Tiber:* this piece holds more of the sentimental than of the enthusiastic spirit of some ode-writers; it breathes notwithstanding an agreeable melancholy, and is in many places affectingly impassioned.
>
> > *Where is the Villa's rural pride,*
> > *The swelling dome's imperial gleam;*
> > *Which lov'd to grace thy verdant side,*
> > *And tremble in thy golden stream?*

Where are the bold, the busy throngs,
  That rush'd impatient to the war,
Or tun'd to peace triumphal songs,
  And hail'd the passing car.

  Along the solitary road*, [*The Flaminian *way.*]
  Th' eternal flint by Consuls trod,
  We muse and mark the sad decays,
  Of mighty works and mighty days.
For these vile wastes, we cry, had fate decreed,
That Veii's *sons should strive, for these* Camillus
                                             bleed!

The conclusion has also a beautiful pathos:

  Tho' from his caves th' unfeeling North,
  Pour'd all his legion'd tempests forth,
    Yet still thy laurel's bloom;
  One deathless glory still remains,
  Thy stream has *roll'd thro'* Latian *plains,*
    Has *wash'd the* walls *of* Rome.

The first elegy, written at the Convent of *Haut Villiers*,
contains a beautiful disuasive from the austerities practiced by
the monks, and after some descriptive imagery, there is a pleasing
generosity in the following sentiment.

  A British bard to Gallia's *fertile shore,*
  Can wish the blessings of eternal peace.

The elegy on the *Mausoleum* of *Augustus* after saying that,

  In ev'ry shrub, in ev'ry flowrets bloom,
    That paints with different hews yon smiling
                                             plain,
  Some hero's ashes issue from the tomb,
    And live a vegetative life again.

he has the following striking thought;

  Perhaps, my Villiers, *for I sing to thee,*
    Perhaps unknowing of the bloom it gives,
  In yon fair Scyon of Apollo's *tree,*
    The sacred dust of young Marcellus *lives.*
  Pluck not the leaf — 'twere sacrilege to wound,
    Th' ideal memory of so sweet a shade;
  In these sad seats an early grave he found,
    And the first rites to gloomy Dis *convey'd.*

The digression to *Marcellus* naturally grows out of this
passage, and is finely closed by recurring to Lord *Villiers*,
with

> *Be thou* Marcellus *with a length of days.*

The elegy to Lord *Newnham* is neatly finished, but has
not many local ideas, and might be written from any other
place as well as *Rome.* [81]

There is nothing very distinctive about the style; the most that can
be said is that Johnson frequently uses such an unadorned style in his
book reviews. [82] The opinions expressed, although not distinctive,
certainly coincide with Johnson's. He believed that odes should be
forceful, enthusiastic, and vigorous. [83] The pleasure that he received
from "an agreeable melancholy" is well known — see, for example,
his praise of *Eloisa to Abelard* in the "Life of Pope" or his choice of
"the most poetical paragraph" in "the whole mass of English poetry"
in his "Life of Congreve." [84] Admittedly, these passages were written
more than twenty years later than the review, but all evidence suggests
that Johnson did not change his basic critical opinions between the
1750's and the 1770's.

It may be argued that the review is laudatory, and that in the only
recorded instance in which Johnson mentioned Whitehead's poetry
he spoke of it unfavorably. [85] He was referring, however, only to
Whitehead's "Birthday Odes" after he had become Poet Laureate.
At the time of Johnson's review Whitehead had not yet succeeded
Cibber, so Johnson's later criticism does not seem pertinent.

The review was reprinted in the *London Chronicle* of February
19–22, 1757, where once more I think I discern the hand of Arthur
Murphy. The review begins: "We were highly pleased (says a judicious
and candid Writer in the Literary Magazine, from whom we borrow
this Article verbatim) to see this Work advertised . . . ." Here again
is the same type of praise, the identical adjectives, and the same manner
of introducing the parenthetical phrase into the midst of a quotation.
I believe that this is Murphy referring once again to Johnson.

Thus, the internal evidence for this review is, at best, neutral. The
opinions expressed are fully consonant with those of Johnson, but
they were also probably consonant with the opinions of a great many
other contemporary readers. The plain, unadorned style was often
used by Johnson in other book reviews, but the use of an undistinctive
prose style is hardly the basis for an attribution of authorship.

Concerning external evidence, we know that Johnson contributed
book reviews to this magazine through the fourteenth monthly issue.
However, since he was not the sole reviewer, is there anything to make

us associate this specific review with Johnson? The answer, I believe, lies in the weight one gives to the evidence of the review in the *London Chronicle*. As one who has spent many months comparing the newspaper and the magazine, I believe that this review is an example of Arthur Murphy's referring to Samuel Johnson in the pages of the *London Chronicle*. I am aware that without demonstrable proof I cannot necessarily expect others to share my belief; perhaps the review may be admitted to the canon tentatively.

[Ch. II, no. 36] *A Letter to a Gentleman in the Country . . .*
  Giving an Authentick and circumstantial Account
  of the Confinement, Behaviour, and Death of
  Admiral Byng

The review begins with this paragraph:

As the trial of Mr. *Byng* has ingrossed a great deal of our conversation for some months past, it may not be amiss to give a summary view of this pamphlet, which relates a number of curious anecdotes of this unhappy gentleman, who has at length paid the forfeit of his life, and fallen a sacrifice to the justice of his country.[86]

The rest of the review consists of extracts and the type of condensations that I find distinctively Johnsonian. For example, in discussing Byng's attitude and behavior before his execution, the pamphlet states:

During all the time of his confinement, his comportment was uniformly the same; almost always chearful, sometimes, with decency, facetious . . . [p. 14].
The nearer approach of death made no change in his manner. He had divine service performed in the morning by the chaplain of the *Monarque*, and usually spent the remainder of the day in conversation with his friends; and sometimes in regulating his private family-affairs, when any thing occurred to his memory as not properly settled agreeable to his intention . . . [pp. 15–16].

The reviewer epitomizes these passages in this manner: "his behaviour was uniformly composed to the last. Divine service was performed for him every morning, and the rest of the day he spent in chearful conversation, and the adjustment of family affairs . . ." (*Literary Magazine*, II, 117).
    One other brief editorial statement occurs in the penultimate paragraph: ". . . it is a remarkable circumstance that the *Ramilles*

broke from her moorings much about the time of execution; which superstitious minds have interpreted various ways."[87]

Since Johnson had already reviewed four pamphlets on Admiral Byng (nos. 25, 26, 29 and 30, above), it is reasonable to suspect that he may have completed the "series" by reviewing this pamphlet on Byng's death.[88] His interest in Byng is unquestioned, and the *Letter* is a very fine pamphlet. It is the only reliable description of Byng's confinement on board HMS *Monarch* and of his behavior when he was sentenced; its detailed accounts are obviously written by an accurate and candid observer. In reviewing the pamphlet, Johnson no longer found occasion for his previous passionate pleading. Byng was dead, and Johnson quietly summarized the one pamphlet which presented a sympathetic and detailed account of the admiral's last days.

The attribution of this review to Johnson is based on the distinctive type of condensations and on its forming part of a unified series, of which Johnson is known to have written the others. As with the review of Whitehead's *Elegies*, I believe this review should be admitted to the canon tentatively.

* * * * *

These, therefore, seem to be Johnson's total output of reviews for the *Literary Magazine*. Some of them are attributed to him on very strong evidence, others on evidence much weaker. The list, I believe, is fairly complete.[89]

CHAPTER II

THE BOOKS JOHNSON REVIEWED
FOR THE *LITERARY MAGAZINE*

Listed below in abbreviated form are all the books which I believe
Johnson reviewed for the *Literary Magazine*. They are arranged in the
order in which they appear in the magazine. If a review was published
in two or three issues, all installments are listed with the first part.
Since Johnson occasionally reviewed more than one book in a review,
I try to avoid confusion by listing each book rather than listing the
reviews. In the case of multi-volume works which were published over
a number of years, only the particular volumes reviewed are listed.

The list is followed by a detailed description of each book. The
order is the same as that in the list; consult Appendix B for a chronological listing of books and pamphlets published during this period.
A complete transcription of the title-page of each book is given, since
in many instances both the *Literary Magazine* and bibliographies (such
as *CBEL*) give such a shortened or distorted form of the title that it is
sometimes difficult to identify the book.

The list of copies for each book is, I hope, accurate but not exhaus-
tive. Each copy I have examined personally is listed with an asterisk.
For all other copies, I have not relied on secondary sources (such as
the NUC) but rather on information from the libraries involved —
correspondence, photocopies of library cards and title-pages, etc.

Literary Magazine, I, no. I (1756).

1. John Armstrong, *The History of the Island of Minorca*
   (pp. 9—14).
2. Stephen White, *Collateral Bee-Boxes* (pp. 27—28).
3. Thomas Birch, *The History of the Royal Society*, v. I—II
   (pp. 30—32).
4. Arthur Murphy, *The Gray's-Inn Journal*, v. I—II (pp. 32—35).
5. Joseph Warton, *Essay on Pope*, v. I (pp. 35—38).
6. James Hampton (trans.), *History of Polybius* (pp. 39—41).

7. Thomas Blackwell, *Memoirs of the Court of Augustus*, v. II (pp. 41—42). Review continued in *LM*, I, no. V (1756), 239—40.

Literary Magazine, I, no. II (1756).

8. Alexander Russell, *The Natural History of Aleppo* (pp. 80—86).
9. Sir Isaac Newton, *Four Letters to Bentley* (pp. 89—91).
10. William Borlase, *Observations on the Islands of Scilly* (pp. 91—97).

Literary Magazine, I, no. III (1756).

11. John Douglas, *Six Letters from A--d B--r* (pp. 126—33).
12. Archibald Bower, *Affidavit* (pp. 126—33).
13. Francis Home, *Experiments on Bleaching* (pp. 136—41).
14. Sir Thomas Browne, *Christian Morals*, 2d ed. (pp. 141—43).
15. Stephen Hales, *An Account of a useful Discovery* (pp. 143—45).

Literary Magazine, I, no. IV (1756).

16. Charles Lucas, *An Essay on Waters* (pp. 167—68).
    Review continued in *LM*, I, no. V (1756), 225—29; review concluded in *LM*, I, no. VI (1756), 288—93.
17. Robert Keith, *A Large New Catalogue of the Bishops of ... Scotland* (pp. 171—76).
18. Patrick Browne, *Civil and Natural History of Jamaica* (pp. 176—85).
19. Charles Parkin, *Account of the Invasion under William Duke of Normandy* (pp. 186—88).
20. *Philosophical Transactions*, Vol. XLIX, Pt. I, for 1755 (pp. 193—97).

Literary Magazine, I, no. V (1756).

21. Johann Georg Keyssler, *Travels through Germany* ... Vol. I, 4° (pp. 240—47).

Literary Magazine, I, no. VI (1756).

22. Mrs. Charlotte Lennox (trans.), *Memoirs of the Duke of Sully* ... 1st ed., 3 vols., 4° (pp. 281—82).
23. Elizabeth Harrison, *Miscellanies* (pp. 282—88).
24. Lewis Evans, *Geographical ... Essays ... the First* — perhaps more commonly known as the *Analysis, Part I* (pp. 293—99).

25. *A Letter to a Member of Parliament ... Relative to the Case of Admiral Byng* (pp. 299–309).
26. John Shebbeare, *An Appeal to the People ... Part I* (pp. 299–309).

Literary Magazine, I, no. VII (1756).

27. Jonas Hanway, *A Journal of Eight Days Journey ...* 1st ed., 4° (pp. 335–42).
28. Samuel Bever, *The Cadet* (p. *343*, misnumbered 335).
29. *Some further Particulars* [re. Byng] (pp. *344–48*, misnumbered 336–40).
30. David Mallet, *The Conduct of the Ministry Impartially Examined* (pp. *348*–51), with pp. *348, 349, 350* misnumbered 340, 341, 342).

Literary Magazine, I, no. IX (1756–57).

31. John Douglas, *Bower and Tillemont compared ...* (pp. 442–53).
32. Archibald Bower, *Answer to a scurrilous Pamphlet ...* (pp. 442–53).
33. Arthur Murphy, Henry Fox, and others, *The Test* (pp. 453–61).
34. Owen Ruffhead, Philip Francis, and others, *The Con-Test* (pp. 453–61).

Literary Magazine, II, no. X (1757).

35. William Whitehead, *Elegies, with an Ode to the Tiber* (p. 31).

Literary Magazine, II, no. XII (1757).

36. *A Letter to a Gentleman in the Country ... Giving an authentick and circumstantial Account of the Confinement, Behaviour, and Death of Admiral Byng* (pp. 116–120).

Literary Magazine, II, no. XIII (1757).

37. Jonas Hanway, *A Journal of Eight Days Journey ...* 2d ed., 2 vols., 8° (pp. *162* [misnumbered 161]–167).
38. Soame Jenyns, *A Free Inquiry into the Nature and Origin of Evil* (pp. 171–75).
    Review continued in *LM*, II, no. XIV (1757), 251–53; review concluded in *LM*, II, no. XV (1757), *299–304* (misnumbered 301–306).

Literary Magazine, II, no. XIV (1757).

   39. Jonas Hanway, A Paper in the *Gazetteer* of May 26, 1757
       (pp. 253–*56* [misnumbered 356]).

1. John Armstrong, d. 1758.

There were two editions of the *History of the Island of Minorca* published in London in the 1750's, and both must be discussed and described here.

First Edition, 1752.

THE / HISTORY / OF THE / ISLAND / OF / *MINORCA*. / By JOHN ARMSTRONG, *Esq*; / ENGINEER in Ordinary to his MAJESTY. / *LONDON:* / Printed for C. DAVIS, opposite *Gray's-Inn,*/ *Holborn*. M.DCC.LII.

Collation: 8°: A⁸ a⁴ b² B—R⁸ S²

Contents: Page *i* half-title, *ii* blank, *iii* title, *iv* blank, *v—vii* Dedication to Richard Offarel, dated *"Chelsea, 30 June* 1752," *viii* blank, ix—xviii Preface, xix—xxvii Contents, *xxviii* "Directions to the Book-binder" and "Errata," 1—243 text, 244—260 Appendix.

There are three plates: Map of Minorca, 1752 (facing title); "Plate of Fossils, with the Coin" (facing p. 143); "Cairn and Heathen-Altar" (facing p. 218).

Press figures: none.

Date of publication: July 30, 1752 (*General Advertiser*; *London Evening-Post*, July 28—30).

Copies: Bodleian; University of British Columbia; British Library (2 copies: 174. b. 30 and 795. e. 39); Library of Congress; Cornell; John Crerar Library; Library Company of Philadelphia; National Library of Scotland; New York Public Library; University of Pennsylvania; Enoch Pratt Free Library, Baltimore; Texas; Yale. Paul Latcham, Hereford.

In the Spring of 1756 it became apparent that Minorca would become a center of conflict between the French and English. Although the formal declaration of war and Admiral Byng's defeat did not occur until May, for several months prior to that time the newspapers were filled with advertisements of various accounts and maps of Minorca. Evidently Lockyer Davis, Armstrong's publisher since the death of his uncle Charles Davis in 1755, decided to take advantage of such interest by reissuing the 1752 edition of the *History*. Whether it was a reissue of the 1752 original sheets with a new title-page, or merely the remaining copies of the 1752 edition, it was advertised as published at least by April 1, 1756 (see the *Daily Advertiser*, which also advertised it on April 4, 6, 8, 10 and 13). Beginning April 26, 1756, the advertisements in the *Daily Advertiser* contain an additional statement:

"to which is added A Letter from an Officer at Minorca, dated the 27th of February last."

Interest in the book was sufficient to call for a new edition. Early in May after Armstrong had completed his slight revisions, he signed and dated his new dedication, "*Chelsea*, 12 *May* 1756." William Bowyer was the printer of the new edition. According to his Paper Stock Ledger (Bodleian MS. DON b. 4, folio 152), he printed 1,000 copies, the first fifty of which he delivered to Davis on May 31, 1756, the same day on which five copies were sent to His Majesty the King. "The Second Edition, with Additions by the Author" was advertised as published on June 5, 1756 (*Public Advertiser*).

Second Edition, 1756.
     THE / HISTORY / OF THE / ISLAND / OF / *MINORCA*. / [rule] / By JOHN ARMSTRONG, *Esq*; / ENGINEER in Ordinary to His MAJESTY. / [rule] / The SECOND EDITION, / With large Additions by the AUTHOR; / Illustrated with COPPER-PLATES. / [double rule] / *LONDON:* / Printed for L. DAVIS, and C. REYMERS,/ against *Gray's-Inn*, *Holborn*. / Printers to the ROYAL SOCIETY. / M.DCC.LVI.

Collation: 8°: A⁸ a⁴ B–R⁸ S⁴

Contents: Page *i* title, *ii* blank, *iii–v* Dedication, *vi* blank, vii–xvi Preface, xvii–xxiv Contents, 1–243 text, 244–260 Appendix, 261–264 Letter from an Officer at Minorca, dated 27 Feb. 1756.

There are five plates: Map of Minorca, 1752 (facing title); Plate II (facing p. 28); III (facing p. 64); IV (facing p. 144); V (facing p. 220).

Press figures: 100–2, 118–2, 125–4, 132–2, 148–4, 166–1.

Date of publication: June 5, 1756 (*Public Advertiser*).

Copies: Academy of Natural Sciences, Philadelphia; Bodleian; British Library (2 copies: 981. b. 26 and G. 16044); Cambridge University Library; Library of Congress; Cornell; Folger; Harvard; Huntington; Indiana (Lilly); Library Company of Philadelphia; U.S. Department of the Navy Library (2 copies); New York Public Library; Syracuse; Texas. Paul Latcham, Hereford; D. D. Eddy.

There are, therefore, four London issues in two editions of Armstrong's *History*: (A) the first edition, 1752; (B) the reissue of the first edition on April 1, 1756; (C) the reissue of the first edition with the additional Letter from Minorca on April 26, 1756 and later; and (D) the second edition on June 5, 1756 and later.

Which version did Johnson review? His review reprints the Letter from an Officer at Minorca, and thus he necessarily reviewed C or D, the only two to contain the Letter. However, Bowyer's ledgers show that no one could have seen a copy of D before May 31, and Johnson's review was published in the first issue of the *Literary Magazine* on May 15. Hence, he reviewed C, which was available at least by April 26.

What is the bibliographical nature of C? Apparently no new title-page was printed for the reissue of B and C in 1756; certainly all copies examined have the original title and text as issued in 1752. The "Letter from an Officer at Minorca," dated 27 Feb. 1756, is a quarter-sheet of octavo, not signed but numbered (1)–(4). Copies of C contain these two leaves inserted in various places, usually at the end of the book; hence, for this issue S^2 of the first edition could be amended to read $S^2 \ T^2$.

Copies of version C: Cambridge University Library (S 582. d. 75. 1); The Public Library of Cincinnati and Hamilton County (Cincinnati, Ohio); Northwestern University. Paul Latcham, Hereford; D. D. Eddy.

Note: All copies of all versions listed above either have been examined by me personally or have been examined by knowledgeable persons and reported to me.

Samuel Johnson's review is in *LM*, I, no. I (1756), 9–14, published May 15, 1756 (*Daily Advertiser*; *London Evening-Post*); it reprints the "Letter from an Officer at Minorca" verbatim (*LM*, pp. 9–10). The first part of the review proper (*LM*, pp. 11–13) is a masterful condensation of material drawn from every section of the book. The only two sections in which Johnson uses quotation marks (*LM*, p. 13) are condensed from pages 26–27 and 28–29.

2. Stephen White

Title: *Collateral* BEE-BOXES. / Or, a New, Easy, and Advantageous / METHOD / OF / MANAGING BEES. / IN WHICH / Part of the HONEY is taken away, in an / easy and pleasant Manner, without de- / stroying, or much disturbing the BEES; / early Swarms, if desired, are encou- / raged, and late ones prevented. / [rule] / By STEPHEN WHITE, M.A. / Rector of *Holton* in *Suffolk*. /

[rule] / [quotation from Ovid] / [double rule] / LONDON, / Printed, and sold by LOCKYER DAVIS, and CHARLES / REYMERS against *Grays-Inn-Gate, Holbourn.* / MDCCLVI.

Collation: 8° (in 4's): A–H⁴

Contents: Page *i* title, *ii* blank, *iii* iv–xii Introduction, *13* 14–63 text, *64* blank. A frontispiece faces the title-page.

Press figures: iv–1, x–1, 21–1, 32–1, 37–4, 44–1, 55–2, 58–4.

Date of publication: March 6, 1756 (*Whitehall Evening Post*, Mar. 4–6, 1756). A second edition was published in 1759 and a third in 1764; copies of these three editions are in Cornell.

Copies: *British Library (2 copies); *Cornell; Yale (Lewis Walpole Library); *D. D. Eddy.

Reviewed by Johnson in *LM*, I, no. I (1756), 27–28; published May 15, 1756 (*Daily Advertiser; London Evening-Post*).

Johnson quotes from pages xii and 57–62 (with omissions). Most of the review consists of a skilled condensation of the entire pamphlet; see Chapter III, below.

3. Thomas Birch, 1705–1766.

Title: THE / HISTORY / OF THE / ROYAL SOCIETY OF LONDON [followed by comma in Vol. II] / FOR IMPROVING OF / NATURAL KNOWLEDGE, / FROM ITS FIRST RISE. / IN WHICH / The most considerable of those Papers communicated to the / SOCIETY, which have hitherto not been published, are inserted in their / proper order, / AS A SUPPLEMENT TO / THE PHILOSOPHICAL TRANSACTIONS./ By THOMAS BIRCH, D.D. / SECRETARY to the ROYAL SOCIETY. / VOL. I. [II] / [Latin quotation from Bacon] / [double rule] / LONDON: / Printed for A. MILLAR in the Strand. / MDCCLVI.

Volume I.

Collation: 4°: *A*⁴ (–*A*4) B–3T⁴

Contents: *A*1ʳ title, *A*1ᵛ blank, *A*2 Dedication, *A*3 The Preface, pages 1–511 text, *512* Errata. Plates are inserted to face pages 70 (in second issue), 78, 136 and 294; see Note, below.

Press figures: $A2^r$–4, 5–8, 7–7, 12–2, 21–4, 22–5, 26–*,
　　28–1, 34–6, 36–1, 42–8, 50–2, 53–4, 62–8, 68–1,
　　71–*, 74–8, 85–6, 94–7, 101–*, 103–1, 107–6, 110–6,
　　119–*, 125–4, 126–7, 133–3, 135–2, 142–7, 150–4,
　　154–6, 168–8, 170–1, 172–*, 184–4, 192–7, 196–8,
　　199–6, 207–4, 210–8, 218–5, 221–2, 228–2, 231–4,
　　234–2, 242–7, 245–8, 250–6, 252–8, 258–2, 260–6,
　　268–7, 274–7, 287–3, 294–6, 298–3, 304–7, 312–8,
　　314–*, 316–1, 322–7, 335–8, 340–7, 348–*, 350–1,
　　354–7, 367–5, 370–5, 380–2, 388–5, 390–7, 398–5,
　　400–4, 407–7, 416–7, 418–2, 421–1, 429–3, 434–8,
　　436–4, 442–3, 444–1, 454–4, 461–5, 463–7, 469–5,
　　474–6, 480–4, 482–8, 488–3, 492–6, 503–6, 506–5,
　　508–6.

Volume II.

Collation: $4°$: A1 (= 3S4?) B–3R^4 3S^4 (–3S4 = A1?)

Contents: A1^r title, A1^v blank, pages 1–501 text, *502* blank.
　　Page 498 misnumbered 984. Plates are inserted to face
　　pages 72, 155 and 258.

Press figures: 7–2, 8–2, 10–2, 16–2, 23–2, 24–2, 26–2,
　　28–2, 34–2, 37–2 [etc.]

Date of publication of Vols. I–II: February 12, 1756 (*Daily
　　Advertiser*; *Public Advertiser*); Vols. III–IV: February 10,
　　1757 (*Daily Advertiser*; *Public Advertiser*). William Strahan
　　printed 750 copies of Vol. I in February, 1756 and 500 copies
　　of Vol. III in December, 1756 (British Library Add. MSS 48800,
　　folio 100).

Copies: Bodleian; British Library (3 copies); *Cambridge University
　　Library (2 copies); *University of Chicago; *Cornell (2 copies);
　　*Harvard (Houghton); Illinois; Rochester; National Library of
　　Scotland; Yale (2 copies); *Sir Geoffrey Keynes (*Bibliotheca
　　Bibliographici*, no. 3626); *D. D. Eddy.

Note: There are two issues of Volume I. The first has only three,
　　numbered plates facing pages 78, 136 and 294. More than
　　a month after the first two volumes had been published, the
　　newspapers advertising the work noted: "A mathematical
　　Scheme omitted in the first Volume will be delivered to those
　　who have already purchased the Book …" (see, for example,
　　the *Public Advertiser*, March 16, 1756). This new, unnumbered
　　plate was inserted facing page 70. The King's dedication copy

in the British Library (128. e. 19—22) lacks the additional plate, but copies of both issues seem equally common: one of the Cambridge copies (Hh. 10. 24—27), the Keynes and Eddy copies, etc. have the additional plate.

Vols. I—II reviewed by Johnson in *LM*, I, no. I (1756), 30—32; published May 15, 1756 (*Daily Advertiser*; *London Evening-Post*). Extracts from Vols. III—IV were printed in *LM*, II, no. XI (1757), 93, but these are reprints of the same extracts that were published in the *London Chronicle* of March 10—12, 1757; there is no reason to associate Samuel Johnson with the reviews of Vols. III—IV.

Johnson quotes from Vol. I, pages 51—52, 199—202. The information in the preliminary paragraphs of Johnson's review is taken from Vol. I, pages 1—4, 16—17. Volume II is neglected.

4. Arthur Murphy, 1727—1805.

Title: THE / GRAY's-INN / JOURNAL. / IN TWO VOLUMES. / VOL. I / [Latin quotation from Sallust] / Eye Nature's Walks, shoot Folly as it flies, / And catch the Manners living, as they rise. / POPE. / LONDON: / Printed by W. FADEN, / FOR / P. VAILLANT, in the Strand. / [rule] / MDCCLVI.

The title-page of Vol. I exists in two states: the first is described above, while the second is the same except for the absence of the fourth line, "IN TWO VOLUMES." The second state was substituted as a cancel (e.g., in the Cornell copy) apparently to make it conform to the title-page of the second volume, which is the same in all respects except for reading "VOL. II." and omitting "IN TWO VOLUMES."

Volume I.

Collation: $12°$: A^6 $B—O^{12}$ P^6 Q^2. B4 missigned B6.

Contents: $A1^r$ title, $A1^v$ blank, $A2^r—A4^r$ Dedication, signed April 5, 1756 by Arthur Murphy, $A4^v$ blank, $A5$ Advertisement, $A6$ Contents (nos. 1—52), pages *1* 2—328 text.

Press figures: 10—3, 21—3, 39—3, 48—3, 50—3, 61—3, 93—3, 94—3, 119—3, 120—3, 130—2, 159—3, 168—3, 191—3, 192—3, 194—3, 205—3, 229—2, 242—3, 261—3, 266—3, 288—3, 299—3, 312—3.

Volume II.

Collation: 12°: A^2 B–P^{12} Q1

Contents: A1^r title, A1^v blank, A2 Contents (nos. 53–104), pages *1* 2–338 text. Page 95 misnumbered 93.

Press figures: 45–3, 50–3, 120–3, 220–2, 239–2, 312–3.

Date of publication: April 14, 1756 (*Public Advertiser*; see the *London Evening-Post*, April 10–13, 13–15, 1756).

Copies: Bodleian; *British Library; *University of Chicago; *Cornell; Huntington; Illinois; Rochester; U.C.L.A. (Clark); *Yale (2 copies; one uncut in the original blue wrappers); *D. D. Eddy.

Reviewed by Johnson in *LM*, I, no. I (1756), 32–35; published May 15, 1756 (*Daily Advertiser*; *London Evening-Post*).

Johnson quotes Vol. II, pages 256–261, which is all of essay no. 93 (dated Sat., July 27, 1754); he omits the True Intelligence section, pages 261–262. This essay about Mirgehan appeared in the original folio edition as no. 43 (dated Sat., July 20, 1754), pages 253–258. The text is revised considerably in the duodecimo edition of 1756.

5. Joseph Warton, 1722–1800.

Title: AN / ESSAY / ON THE / WRITINGS [red] / AND / GENIUS [red] / OF / POPE. / [rule] / [quotation from Quintilian] / [rule] / *LONDON:* [red] / PRINTED FOR M. COOPER, AT THE GLOBE IN PATER-NOSTER ROW. / [rule] / MDCCLVI.

Collation: 8° (in 4's): A^4 b^2 B–2U^4

Contents: Page *i* title, *ii* blank, *iii* iv–xii Dedication, *1* 2–334 text, *335–336* blank.

Press figures: none.

Date of publication: March 26, 1756 (*Public Advertiser*; *London Evening-Post*).

Copies: Bodleian; *British Library; *Cornell; Huntington; Illinois (2 copies); Pennsylvania State University; U.C.L.A. (Clark); Yale (2 copies); *D. D. Eddy; *Cambridge University Library.

Reviewed by Johnson in *LM*, I, no. I (1756), 35–38; published May 15, 1756 (*Daily Advertiser*; *London Evening-Post*).

Johnson quotes from pages 4, 10, 37, 52, 53, 63–64, 142, 149, 150, 203, 334; he paraphrases many other pages.

6. Polybius.

Title: THE / GENERAL HISTORY / OF / POLYBIUS. / IN FIVE BOOKS. / Translated from the GREEK / By Mr. HAMPTON. / LONDON: / Printed by J. HUGHS, / For R. and J. DODSLEY in Pall-Mall. / MDCCLVI.

Collation: $4°$: A^4 a^4 b^2 B–$4B^4$

Contents: Page *i* title, *ii* blank, *iii* iv–xx Preface, *1* 2–104 text of Book I, *105* 106–186 text of Book II, *187* 188–329 text of Book III, *330* blank, *331* 332–438 text of Book IV, *439* 440–559 text of Book V, *560* Errata. Two folding maps are inserted facing pages 1 and 105.

Press figures: 15–1, 406–2, 424–1, 432–2, 536–3, 542–3.

Note: The collation and contents listed above are of the first issue of the book (copies: British Library, Cornell and D. D. Eddy). More than a year after the book was first published, an eight-page index was printed and issued gratis; see the *Daily Advertiser* of March 26, 1757. The Newberry Library and Cambridge University Library copies have the index.

Date of publication: March 13, 1756 (*Daily Advertiser*; *Public Advertiser*).

Copies: Bodleian; *British Library; *Cambridge University Library; *Cornell (2 copies); Huntington; Illinois; *Newberry Library; Yale; *D. D. Eddy.

Reviewed by Johnson in *LM*, I, no. I (1756), 39–41; published May 15, 1756 (*Daily Advertiser*; *London Evening-Post*).

Johnson quotes from pages 278–83.

Note: On April 26, 1755 Robert Dodsley signed a contract with James Hampton to purchase the copyright of his translation of the first five books of Polybius for two hundred fifty guineas. Hampton was to furnish the printer with copy within one month of the agreement so that the work might be printed, together with a Preface and Index, by December 29, 1755. Hampton also was to correct the sheets as they were printed. Dodsley was to pay fifty guineas on delivery of the copy for the first three books — Hampton's receipt for this amount is dated June 14, 1755 — and to pay the remainder on the day of publication. Hampton's final receipt is dated March 9, 1756; the book was advertised as published on March 13, 1756.

This is a short summary of the original two-page document in Boston Public Library (Ch. G. 13. 7).

7. Thomas Blackwell, 1701–1757.

Title: MEMOIRS / Of the COURT of / *AUGUSTUS*. / By THOMAS BLACKWELL, J.U.D. / PRINCIPAL of MARISHAL COLLEGE in the UNIVERSITY / OF *ABERDEEN*. / VOL. II. / [quotation from Lucan] / *EDINBURGH:* / Printed by HAMILTON, BALFOUR and NEILL. / M,DCC,LV.

Collation of Vol. II: 4°: π^6 A–3L^4

Contents of Vol. II: Page *i* title, *ii* blank, *iii* Contents, *iv–v* quotation from Polybius, *vi*–vii Preface, *viii* blank, *ix–xi* Dedication, *xii* "Advertisement," *1* 2–53 *54* 55–103 *104* 105–191 *192* 193–379 *380* 381–456 text. Pages 33–40 misnumbered 25–32, and 350–351 misnumbered 450–451. Plates are inserted facing pages 77, 111, 204, 227, 327, 342, 349 and 360.

Press figures: none.

Date of publication of Vol. II: in Edinburgh, Feb. 1756 (*Scots Magazine*, xviii [Feb., 1756], 112); in London, Feb. 2, 1756 (*Daily Advertiser*).

Copies: *Bodleian (2 copies); British Library (2 copies); *Cambridge University Library; *Library of Congress; *Cornell; *National Library of Scotland; Yale (2 copies); *D. D. Eddy.

Reviewed by Johnson in *LM*, I, no. I (1756), 41–42, published May 15, 1756 (*Daily Advertiser*; *London Evening-Post*) and I, no. V (1756), 239–240, published Sept. 15, 1756 (*Public Advertiser*).

All of Johnson's quotations are from Book V of Vol. II, page 1–53.

Note: This work by Thomas Blackwell, the younger (1701–57), was published in three volumes over the course of a decade. Vol. I, containing Books I–IV, was published in 1753 (Edinburgh: Hamilton, Balfour and Neill). The second volume, described

above, contains Books V—IX. The last volume, containing
Books X—XV, appeared in 1763 (London: A. Millar).

8. Alexander Russell, 1715?—1768.

Title: THE / NATURAL HISTORY / OF / ALEPPO, / AND /
PARTS ADJACENT. / CONTAINING / A DESCRIPTION of
the CITY, and the Principal / NATURAL PRODUCTIONS in
its Neighbourhood; / TOGETHER WITH / An Account of the
CLIMATE, INHABITANTS, and DISEASES; / particularly
of the PLAGUE, with the Methods used by the / EUROPEANS
for their Preservation. / By ALEX. RUSSELL, M.D. / [double
rule] / LONDON: / Printed for A. MILLAR, in the Strand. /
MDCCCLVI. [sic]

Collation: 4°: A^4 B—2M^4 2N^2

Contents: Page *i* title, *ii* blank, *iii* dedication to Alexander Drummond,
iv blank, *v* vi—viii Advertisement, *1* 2—144 *145* 146—189 *190*
191—223 text, *224* blank, *225* 226—261 *262* 263—266 text,
267—275 index, *276* errata. Page 139 misnumbered 138.
      Sixteen numbered folding plates are inserted as follows:
1 (facing p. 33); 2, 3, 4 (facing p. 34); 5 (facing p. 41);
6 (facing p. 44); 7 (facing p. 46); 8 (facing p. 47); 9 (facing
p. 64); 10 (facing p. 71); 11 (facing p. 72); 12 (facing p. 73);
13 (facing p. 76); 14 (facing p. 95); 15 (facing p. 100); and
16 (facing p. 101).
      In addition, some copies have another unnumbered folding
plate which was issued more than a year after the book was
first published. On July 22, 1757 the *Daily Advertiser*
announced that the book now contained an additional plate
of the Aleppo sheep and goat which "will be delivered to
former purchasers of the book." Marked to be inserted facing
page 52, it is present in the Library of Congress and D. D. Eddy
copies.

Press figures: *v*—8, vi—2, 2—1, 4—*, 12—8, 18—6, 20—4, 28—4, 38—7,
46—6, 55—4, 62—*, 64—2, 66—5, 72—8, 74—8, 80—2, 87—1,
88—3, 94—3, 102—7, 111—6, 116—5, 127—6, 130—8, 138—2,
152—3, 154—8, 167—4, 175—3, 180—2, 194—9, 208—5, 215—2,
220—3, 228—9, 231—6, 234—1, 237—6, 245—4, 246—3, 250—*,
253—9, 258—3, *268*—4, *271*—3, *274*—4.

Date of publication: May 5, 1756 (*Daily Advertiser*; *Public Advertiser*).

William Strahan printed 500 copies of this book in May, 1756 (British Library Add. MSS 48800, folio 100).

Copies: *Bodleian; *British Library; *Cambridge University Library; *Library of Congress; *Cornell; Illinois; Kansas; Yale (2 copies); *D. D. Eddy.

Reviewed by Johnson in *LM*, I, no. II (1756), 80–86; published June 15, 1756 (*Public Advertiser*). Johnson quotes from pages 93 and 117, but most of the review is a skillful paraphrase and abridgement.

9. Sir Isaac Newton, 1642–1727.

Title: FOUR / LETTERS / FROM / SIR ISAAC NEWTON / TO / DOCTOR BENTLEY. / CONTAINING / SOME ARGUMENTS / IN / PROOF of a DEITY. / [ornament] / LONDON: / Printed for R. and J. DODSLEY, *Pall-Mall*, / [rule] / MDCCLVI.

Collation: 8° (in 4's): A^2 B–E^4 F^2

Contents: $A1^r$ half-title, $A1^v$ blank, $A2^r$ title, $A2^v$ blank, pages 1–11 text of first letter, *12* blank, 13–21 text of second letter, *22* blank, 23–35 text of third and fourth letters, *36* blank. In the British Library copy, the half-title follows the title.

Press figures: none.

Date of publication: May 12, 1756 (*Public Advertiser*).

Copies: *Bodleian (lacks half-title); *British Library; *Harvard (Houghton; lacks half-title); Illinois; *King's College, Cambridge (Keynes F. 6. 14; uncut, with the half-title); Rochester; St. John's College, Cambridge; Trinity College, Cambridge; *Yale; Sir Geoffrey Keynes (*Bibliotheca Bibliographici*, no. 3288).

Reviewed by Johnson in *LM*, I, no. II (1756), 89–91; published June 15, 1756 (*Public Advertiser*).

Johnson quotes from pages 2–3, 14–15, 33–34.

10. William Borlase, 1695–1772.

Title: OBSERVATIONS / ON THE / Ancient and Present State / OF THE / ISLANDS OF SCILLY, / And their Importance to the / TRADE of *GREAT-BRITAIN*. / In a LETTER to the

Reverend / CHARLES LYTTELTON, LL.D. / Dean of EXETER, and F.R.S. / [rule] / *By* WILLIAM BORLASE, *M.A. F.R.S.* / [rule] / *OXFORD:* / PRINTED BY W. JACKSON. / Sold by W. SANDBY, in *Fleetstreet*, and R. BALDWIN, in *Pater-noster* / *Row, London*; Mess. FLETCHER, CLEMENTS, and PARKER, in *Oxford*; / Mess. LEAKE and FREDERICK at *Bath*; Mess. SCORE and THORN / at *Exeter*; and Mess. JEWELL and MICHELL in *Cornwall.* / [rule] / M.D.CC.LVI.

Collation: 4°: A^2 B–S^4 T^2

Contents: $A1^r$ half-title, $A1^v$ blank, $A2^r$ title, $A2^v$ blank, pages *1* 2–140 text. There are five handsomely engraved plates. Plate II is printed on page 19; the others are folding plates, inserted as follows: I, facing p. 1; III, p. 40; IV, p. 43; and V, p. 47.

Press figures: none.

Date of publication: January 20, 1756 (*Public Advertiser*; *London Evening-Post*).

Copies: *Bodleian (3 copies); *British Library (3 copies); *Cambridge University Library; *Cornell; Huntington; Kansas; *Newberry Library; *National Library of Scotland; Yale; *D. D. Eddy.

Reviewed by Johnson in *LM*, I, no. II (1756), 91–97; published June 15, 1756 (*Public Advertiser*). Johnson quotes from pages 4–5, 17–18, 23–24, 25–26, 28–29, 51, 54–55, 58–61, 87–92, 119–124, 132–133, 135, 137, 139. He paraphrases and adapts pages 5–16, 18–23, 28.

11. John Douglas, 1721–1807.

Title: SIX / LETTERS / FROM / A——d B——r / TO / Father SHELDON, [Italic] / Provincial of the *Jesuits* in *England*; / Illustrated with / Several REMARKABLE FACTS, / tending to ascertain the *Authenticity* / of the said LETTERS, and the true / *Character* of the WRITER. / [rule] / [quotation] / [double rule] / LONDON: / Printed for J. MORGAN, in *Pater-noster Row*, / M DCC LVI. / [Price Eighteen-pence.]

Collation: 8°: $\pi1$ (= G4) A–F^8 G^4 (–G4 = $\pi1$)

Contents: $\pi1^r$ title, $\pi1^v$ blank, pages 1–92 text, *93* special title for the Appendix, *94* blank, 95–101 text of the Appendix, *102* Erratum.

Press figures: none.

Date of publication: June 28, 1756 (*Public Advertiser*; *Whitehall Evening Post*, June 26–29).

Copies: *Bodleian (2 copies); British Library; *Cambridge University Library (2 copies); *University of Chicago; Columbia; Library of Congress; *Cornell; Harvard (Houghton); Huntington; Illinois; Indiana; *National Library of Scotland; *Newberry Library; New York Public Library; Texas; Wayne State University; *Yale; *D. D. Eddy (2 copies).

Reviewed by Johnson in *LM*, I, no. III (1756), 126–133; published July 15, 1756 (*Public Advertiser*). Johnson quotes from pages 4–7, 74–78, 80–81, 85–87. This is a double review; Johnson reviewed it with Bower's *Affidavit* . . . London: W. Sandby, 1756 (see next item).

12. Archibald Bower, 1686–1766.

Title: Mr. *Archibald Bower*'s / AFFIDAVIT / In Answer to the / FALSE ACCUSATION / Brought against him by / *PAPISTS.* / To which are added, / I. A Circumstantial NARRATIVE of what hath / since passed between Mr. *Bower* and Sir *Henry* / *Bedingfeld* in relation thereto. / II. Copies of the said pretended Letters sent him / by Sir *Henry Bedingfeld*, and of a subsequent / Affidavit made by Mr. *Bower of their not* / *being wrote by him, or with his Privity.* / WITH SOME / Short OBSERVATIONS on those pretended Letters, / proving them to be *Spurious.* / [double rule] / *LONDON:* / Printed for W. SANDBY, at the *Ship*, opposite / *St. Dunstan*'s Church, *Fleet-street.* / [short rule] / MDCCLVI.

Collation: 8° (in 4's): π1 A–F⁴ G1

Contents: π1ʳ title, π1ᵛ blank, pages 1–37 text, *38* 39–48 Appendix, 49 Postscript, dated June 30, 1756, *50* blank.

Press figures: 6–5, 15–8, 18–4, 26–5, 46–8.

Date of publication: July 1, 1756 (*Daily Advertiser*).

Copies: *Bodleian; British Library; *Cambridge University Library (3 copies); Library of Congress; *Cornell; *Harvard (Houghton); Huntington; *National Library of Scotland; New York Public Library; Princeton; Texas; *Yale; *D. D. Eddy.

Reviewed by Johnson in *LM*, I, no. III (1756), 126–133; published July 15, 1756 (*Public Advertiser*). Johnson quotes from pages

21–30, 36–37, 33–34. This is a double review; Johnson reviewed it with Douglas' *Six Letters* . . . London: J. Morgan, 1756 (see preceding item).

13. Francis Home, 1719–1813.

Title: EXPERIMENTS / ON / BLEACHING. / By FRANCIS HOME, M.D. / Fellow of the Royal College of Physicians in *Edinburgh*./ [Greek quotation] / *EDINBURGH:* / Printed by SANDS, DONALDSON, MURRAY, & COCHRAN. / For A. KINCAID and A. DONALDSON. / MDCCLVI.

Collation: 8° (in 4's): π^4 (−π4 = 2T1?) A–2S^4 2T1 (= π4?)

Contents: Page *i* title, *ii* blank, *iii* Advertisement, *iv* v–vi A general plan of the work, *1* 2–36 *37* 38–330 text.

Press figures: none.

Date of publication: in Edinburgh, Jan. 1756 (*Scots Magazine*, xviii [Jan., 1756], 56); in London, Feb. 11, 1756 (*Public Advertiser*).

Copies: *Bodleian; *British Library; *Cambridge University Library; *Cornell; *National Library of Scotland (2 copies); New York Public Library; *Yale; *D. D. Eddy.

Reviewed by Johnson in *LM*, I, no. III (1756), 136–141; published July 15, 1756 (*Public Advertiser*). Johnson quotes from pages 21–26, 26–35, 224–225, 227, 228, 229–230, 232–233, 235–236, 237–238, 238–239, 240–241, 249, 252, 295, 297–298, 299–300.

14. Sir Thomas Browne, 1605–1682.

Title: CHRISTIAN / MORALS: / BY / Sir THOMAS BROWNE, / Of NORWICH, M.D. / AND AUTHOR OF / RELIGIO MEDICI. / THE SECOND EDITION. / WITH / A LIFE OF THE AUTHOR, / BY / *SAMUEL JOHNSON*; / AND / EXPLANATORY NOTES. / *LONDON:* / Printed by RICHARD HETT, / For J. PAYNE, at POPE'S HEAD, in / PATER-NOSTER ROW. / MDCCLVI.

Collation: 8°: A^2 a–d^8 B–I^8 K^4

Contents: $A1^r$ half-title, $A1^v$ blank, $A2^r$ title, $A2^v$ blank, pages *i* ii–lxi Johnson's "Life of Sir Thomas Browne," *lxii–lxiv* blank,

1 special title to Browne's *Christian Morals*, *2* blank, *3–4* dedication, *5–6* Preface, 7 8–52 *53* 54–81 *82* 83–136 text.

Press figures: none.

Date of publication: March 18, 1756 (*Public Advertiser*; *London Evening-Post*).

Copies: *Bodleian; British Library (2 copies); *University of Chicago; *Cornell; Harvard (Houghton); Huntington; Illinois; Kansas; *Pembroke College, Cambridge; Rochester; U.C.L.A. (Clark); Yale; *D. D. Eddy.

Reviewed by Johnson in *LM*, I, no. III (1756), 141–143; published July 15, 1756 (*Public Advertiser*).

Johnson quotes the whole last part of his life of Browne, pages lii–lxi.

15. Stephen Hales, 1677–1761.

Title: AN / ACCOUNT / OF A / USEFUL DISCOVERY / TO / Distill double the usual Quantity of SEA- / WATER, by blowing Showers of AIR up / through the DISTILLING LIQUOR; / AND ALSO / To have the DISTILLED WATER perfectly fresh / and good by means of a little Chalk. / AND / An Account of the great Benefit of VENTILATORS / in many Instances, in preserving the HEALTH and / LIVES of People, in Slave and other Transport Ships; / which were read before the ROYAL SOCIETY. / ALSO / An Account of the good Effect of blowing Showers of / AIR up through MILK, thereby to cure the ill Taste / which is occasioned by some Kinds of Food of Cows. / [rule] / By *STEPHEN HALES*, D.D. F.R.S. / Member of the Royal Society of Sciences at *Paris*, / AND / Clerk of the Closet to Her ROYAL HIGHNESS / the PRINCESS of *Wales*. / [double rule] / *LONDON:* / Printed for RICHARD MANBY, in the *Old-Bailey*, / near *Ludgate-Hill*. M.DCC.LVI.

Collation: 8°: A–C^8 D^4 E^2

Contents: Page *1* title, *2* blank, 3–58 text, 59 "Explanation of the Figures," *60* Advertisements. A plate is inserted between E1 and E2. Page 47 is misnumbered 45 in the British Library copy.

Press figures: 14–1, 16–4, 18–4, 24–3, 26–4, 38–3, 40–3, 48–3, 56–3. This book is remarkable for having three press figures in the B and C gatherings, with no cancelled leaves. Figure 26—4, however, is lacking in the British Library copies of both the first and "second" editions.

Date of publication: February 3, 1756 (*Public Advertiser*; *Whitehall Evening Post*, Feb. 3—5).

Copies: *Bodleian; *British Library; New York Public Library; *Yale Medical Historical Library.

Reviewed by Johnson in *LM*, I, no. III (1756), 143—145, published July 15, 1756 (*Public Advertiser*). Johnson quotes from pages 4—5, 11, 13, 19, 39—41, 51—52, 54, 57—58.

Note: A second edition of this work was published by Manby in 1756. It is a reissue of first edition sheets, with the following exceptions: it has a new title-page, reading "The Second Edition," and it has "An Appendix" of seven leaves inserted between E1 and E2. These new leaves are signed E2, E3, and E4. The plate is inserted between the D and E gatherings. (Copies: *Bodleian; New York Public Library.)

16.   Charles Lucas, 1713—1771.

Title: AN / ESSAY / ON / WATERS. / IN THREE PARTS. / TREATING, / I. Of SIMPLE WATERS. / II. Of COLD, MEDICATED WATERS. / III. Of NATURAL BATHS. / By C. LUCAS, M.D. / [Greek and Latin quotations] / [double rule] / LONDON, / Printed for A. MILLAR, in the Strand. / MDCCLVI.

Part I.

Collation: $8°$: A^8 a^8 b^4 $B—P^8$ Q^4

Contents: Page *i* title, *ii* blank, *iii* iv—xiv dedication "to his royal highness the Prince," *xv* xvi—xxviii preface, *xxix* xxx—xxxv contents, *xxxvi* blank, *xxxvii—xxxviii* errata, *xxxix* dedication to the Earl of Macclesfield, *xl* blank, 1—232 text.

Press figures: xv—4, xxx—2 or none, 2—4, 4—1, 28—3, 42—5, 45—3, 54—7, 57—8, 78—2, 96—2, 108—7, 120—8, 139—2, 157—4, 162—*, 173—1, 191—5, 205—5, 223—5, 228—6 or none.

Inserted plates: none.

for the Literary Magazine 49

Part II.

Collation: 8°: $A1$ a^2 b^4 B^4 C–S^8 T^8 $(-T6, 7, 8 = A1$ a^2?)

Contents: Page *i* part title, *ii* blank, *iii* iv–xiv contents, *1* 2–274 text (with many pages unnumbered).

Press figures: xii–2, 8–7, 14–8, 42–2, 65–3, 71–7, 82–7, 92–6, 106–2, 133–5, 134–8, 142–1, 149–6, 154–5, 170–8, 200–6, 202–1, 213–3, *226*–3, 228–6, 247–3, 258–3, 266–4.

Plate I inserted facing p. 89.

Part III.

Collation: 8°: B^8 ($B1 + b^8 + B2$–8) C–$2A^8$.

Contents: Page *i* part title, *ii* blank, *iii* iv–xiii Contents, *xiv* blank, *xv–xvi* Errata for Part III, *xvii–xviii* Errata for Part II, then, beginning on B2, *iii* iv–vii Dedication to the Earl of Shelburne, 8–206 text (with many pages unnumbered), *207* section title, *208* blank, *ccix* ccx–ccxvii Dedication to the Earl of Chesterfield, *218* blank, 219–368 text (with many pages unnumbered). Page 18 misnumbered 106; 351 misnumbered 531.

Plate II inserted facing p. 222.

Press figures: 10–3, 20–4, 38–4, 50–8, 80–8, 94–7, 98–8, 122–5, 139–4, 158–9, 164–9, 178–8, 192–7, 196–4, ccx–7, 224–6, 233–2, 244–6 or 8, *254*–4, 260–1, 270–2, 276–1, 286–*, 303–2, 316–2, 328–3, 335–*, 349–*, 350–5, 358–2.

Date of publication: April 8, 1756 (*Public Advertiser*; *London Evening-Post*). William Strahan printed 500 copies of this book in March, 1756 (British Library Add. MSS 48800, folio 100).

Copies: *Bodleian; *British Library; Library of Congress (Parts I and II only); Illinois; University of Massachusetts, Amherst; *U.S. National Library of Medicine; New York Academy of Medicine, New York; College of Physicians of Philadelphia; *D. D. Eddy.

Reviewed by Johnson in *LM*, I, no. IV (1756), 167–168, published August 16, 1756 (*Daily Advertiser*); and in *LM*, I, no. V (1756), 225–229, published Sept. 15, 1756 (*Public Advertiser*); and in *LM*, I, no. VI (1756), 288–293, published Oct. 15, 1756 (*Daily Advertiser*; *Public Advertiser*).

Johnson quotes from Part I, pages 23–24, 53, 81–83, 83–84, 84–86,
86–88, 135–136, 138, 193–199; Part III, pages 259–263, 273,
281–283, 333, 335–336, 337–338, 339–341.

17. Robert Keith, 1681–1757.

Title: A LARGE NEW / CATALOGUE / OF THE / BISHOPS of the
several SEES / Within the KINGDOM of *SCOTLAND*, / Down
to the YEAR 1688. / Instructed by proper and authentic
VOUCHERS: / TOGETHER WITH / Some other THINGS
necessary to the better KNOWLEDGE of the / *Ecclesiastical
State* of this KINGDOM in former Times: / AS ALSO, / A brief
PREFACE concerning the first planting of CHRISTIANITY in
Scot- / *land*, and the State of that CHURCH in the earlier AGES. /
EDINBURGH: / Printed by THO. and WAL. RUDDIMANS,
and sold by the Book- / sellers in Town. M.D.CC.LV.

Collation: 4° (in 2's): π^4 ($-\pi4 = X1$)· a–e² A–30² 3Pl + X1 + 3P2
3Q–4G² = 166 leaves.

Contents: $\pi1^r$ title, $\pi1^v$ blank, $\pi2^r$ dedication, $\pi2^v$ blank, $\pi3^r$ Advertisement, $\pi3^v$ blank, pages *i* ii–xx Preface, *1* 2–180, 173–234
text of Keith's *Catalogue*, X1ʳ special title of "An Account of
all the Religious Houses that were in Scotland at the Time of
the Reformation . . ." by John Spotiswood of Spotiswood,
X1ᵛ blank, *235* 236–293 text, *294* 295–296 Index to
Spotiswood's "Account." The first page of each of the numerous
sections is not numbered. Page 152 misnumbered 521; all pages
misnumbered after page 180.

Press figures: none.

Date of publication: in Edinburgh, Nov. 1755 (*Scots Magazine*, xvii
[Nov., 1755], 568); in London, June 17, 1756 (*London
Evening-Post*).

Copies: *Bodleian (3 copies); *British Library; *Cambridge Univer-
sity Library; *Cornell; Folger; Harvard; *National Library of
Scotland (2 copies); *Westminster Theological Seminary,
Philadelphia; *D. D. Eddy.

Reviewed by Johnson in *LM*, I, No. IV (1756), 171–176; published
Aug. 16, 1756 (*Daily Advertiser*; *Public Advertiser*). Johnson
quotes from pages 158–160 and 41–45 in his review.

Note: Proposals for printing this book by subscription were issued on two quarto leaves dated "June 20th, 1753." Each subscriber initially paid 2s.; the subscriber to pay, when the book was printed, ". . . what further remains to make up Three-half-pence Sterling only for each Sheet of the Book."

I have located two copies of these proposals, one in the Bodleian (Adds. Scotland. 4°. 148) and one in the National Library of Scotland (MS. 8888).

18. Patrick Browne, 1720?–1790.

Title: THE / CIVIL and NATURAL / HISTORY / OF /*JAMAICA.* / In Three PARTS. / CONTAINING, / I. An accurate Description of that Island, its Situation and Soil; / with a brief Account of its former and present State, Government, / Revenues, Produce, and Trade. / II. A History of the natural Productions, including the various Sorts / of native Fossils; perfect and imperfect Vegetables; Quadrupedes, / Birds, Fishes, Reptiles and Insects; with their Properties and Uses / in Mechanics, Diet, and Physic. / III. An Account of the Nature of Climates in general, and their / different Effects upon the human Body; with a Detail of the / Diseases arising from this Source, particularly within the Tropics. / In Three DISSERTATIONS. / The Whole illustrated with Fifty *Copper-Plates:* / In which the most curious Productions are represented of the natural Size, and / delineated immediately from the Objects. / [rule] / *By* PATRICK BROWNE, *M.D.* / [double rule] / LONDON: / Printed for the AUTHOR; and sold by T. OSBORNE, and J. SHIPTON, / in *Gray's-Inn.* MDCCLVI.

Collation: 2°: A^2 a² B–6N² *60* 1

Contents: *A*1ʳ half-title, *A*1ᵛ blank, *A*2ʳ title, *A*2ᵛ quotation, pages *i–ii* Dedication, *iii–iv* List of Subscribers, v–viii Preface, 1–27 text of Part I, 28 blank, *29* special title, *30* quotation, xxxi–xxxiv Preface, 35–66 text of Part II Book I, *67* special title, *68* quotation, *lxix*–lxx Preface, 71–374 text of Part II Book II, *375* special title, *376* quotation, *ccclxxvii* ccclxxviii (misnumbered ccclxxvii)–ccclxxix Preface, *380* blank, 381–490 text of Part II Book III, *491* 492–503 index, *504* blank, *505–506* "A Catalogue of the Authors whose Names are abbreviated in this Work." [N.B. The location of this last, unsigned leaf varies in some copies.]

Page 242 misnumbered as 342; 243 as 343; and ccclxxviii as ccclxxvii.

In addition there are inserted a map of Jamaica, a chart of Port Royal, and full-page plates nos. 1–38 of flora and 39–49 of fauna. Locations of all of these vary in different copies.

A third part is called for by the title-page, but this was not included. In a note on page 490, Browne says the book is already too big to add Part III; he will print it, he says, in a small octavo "in the ensuing season." Evidently this volume was never published.

Except for the expected variations in binding of the inserted, illustrative material, all of the copies listed (except one) are identical in their printed pages. The exception is British Library copy 1789. d. 7, whose pages 1–12 (the C, D and E gatherings) present a greatly different text in a totally different setting of type. Collation shows that these are the sheets of the 1789 edition; they are easily identified because they have no press figures, while the C, D and E gatherings of the 1756 edition have press figures (as listed below).

Press figures: 4–2, 6–1, 11–2, 12–4, 56–3, 138–2, 143–1, 144–1, 147–2, 149–1, 156–2, 163–3, 164–2, 165–1, 167–1, 172–3, 174–2, 176–4, 178–1, 180–4, 183–4, 184–1, 187–2, 190–4, 195–1, 196–4, 198–4, 204–1, 207–4, 210–1, 214–1, 216–2, 220–3, 224–3, 227–2, 231–2, 232–4, 235–1, 236–4, 238–2, 240–4, 243 (misnumbered 343)–4, 244–2, 246–2, 248–1, 252–1, 255–4, 258–1, 264–1, 266–1, 268–2, 270–1, 275–2, 278–2, 282–2, 284–4, 286–2, 288–1, 290–4, 295–2, 298–1, 300–2, 303–2, 304–4, 308–1, 310–1, 314–1, 319–4, 320–1, 322–2, 327–1, 332–4, 340–1, 344–2, 346–1, 348–4, 350–1, 352–2, 354–1, 356–2, 360–4, 363–1, 368–4, 371–1, 372–2, ccclxxviii (misnumbered ccclxxvii)–4, 382–1, 386–4, 392–4, 395–4, 400–3, 403–4, 406–1, 408–2, 410–4, 416–4, 418–4, 423–2, 428–4, 431–4 or none, 432–2, 434–1, 438–4, 444–2, 447–1, 454–4, 458–1, 462–4, 467–2, 468–4, 472–4, 476–1, 478–4, 480–1, 484–1, 486–3, *491*–4, 492–1, 494–1, 496–2, 498–2, 503–3, *505*–4.

William Bowyer was the printer of this book. Information in his Paper Stock Ledger (Bodleian MS DON b. 4, folio 147) shows that 750 copies were printed, 12 on Demy, 738 on Crown. The volume did not have a large sale: only 254 copies were distributed in the first two years after publication, and Bowyer's ledger shows that on May 26, 1758 he sold the remaining copies. When a "second" edition was issued in 1789 (London: B. White and Son), it included a new half-title, title-page, four additional indexes, and a new map of Jamaica, but press figures indicate that the sheets (except C, D and E) are of the 1756 edition. The Cornell and National Library of Scotland copies of the 1789 edition even include the 1756 list of subscribers. One British Library copy of the 1756 edition (459. c. 4) has bound at the back of the volume all of the new material printed in 1789 except the map.

Date of publication: March 18, 1756 (*Daily Advertiser; Public Advertiser*).

The folio volume sold for two guineas, in sheets. However, within two months of publication, some special copies were advertised: "A few Copies, very elegantly coloured under the Inspection of the Author, will be sold at three Guineas and a half each, in Sheets" (see, for example, the *Public Advertiser* of May 6, 1756).
I have not located any colored copy.

Copies: *British Library (2 copies); *John Carter Brown; *Library of Congress; Illinois; *New York Public Library; *D. D. Eddy.

Reviewed by Johnson in *LM*, I, no. IV (1756), 176–185; published August 16, 1756 (*Daily Advertiser; Public Advertiser*). Johnson quotes from pages 129–133, 156–157, 214, 247–248, 283, 419, 423–424, 432–433, 461, 463.

19. Charles Parkin, 1689–1765.
Title: AN / IMPARTIAL ACCOUNT / OF THE / INVASION / UNDER / WILLIAM Duke of NORMANDY, / And the CONSEQUENCES of it: / With proper REMARKS. / Humbly offered to the Consideration of the NOBILITY, / GENTRY, CLERGY and COMMONALTY of GREAT BRI- / TAIN, particularly to those of the County of NORFOLK. / [rule] / By *CHARLES PARKIN*, A.M. / Rector of *Oxburgh* in *Norfolk*. / [rule] / [Latin quotation from Cicero] / [double rule] / *LONDON:* / Printed by E. OWEN, near *Chancery-Lane:* / For THOMAS TRYE, near *Gray's-Inn-Gate, Holborn.* 1756.

Collation: 4°: A^2 B–E^4 F^2

Contents: $A1^r$ half-title, $A1^v$ blank, $A2^r$ title, $A2^v$ blank, pages 1–36 text.

Press figures: none.

Date of publication: May 12, 1756 (*Daily Advertiser; Public Advertiser*).

Copies: *Bodleian; *British Library; *Library of Congress; *D. D.
Eddy. Only the Bodleian copy has the half-title.

Reviewed by Johnson in *LM*, I, no. IV (1756), 186—188; published
August 16, 1756 (*Daily Advertiser*; *Public Advertiser*). Johnson
quotes from pages 30—34.

20. Title: PHILOSOPHICAL / TRANSACTIONS, / GIVING SOME /
ACCOUNT / OF THE / Present Undertakings, Studies, *and*
Labours, / OF THE / INGENIOUS, / IN MANY / Considerable
Parts of the WORLD. / [rule] / VOL. XLIX. PART I. For the
Year 1755. / [rule] / *LONDON*. / Printed for L. DAVIS and
C. REYMERS, / Printers to the ROYAL SOCIETY, / against
Gray's-Inn Gate, in *Holbourn*. / [short rule] / M.DCC.LVI.
(The title-page is enclosed with double rules on all four sides.)

Collation: 4° (with vertical chain lines): a—b⁴ B—3K⁴ 3L²

Contents: a1ʳ title, a1ᵛ blank, a2ʳ—b4ᵛ Contents, pages 1—444 text.
Many plates are inserted.

Press figures: b3ʳ—5, 2—1, 22—1, 30—2, 40—4, 47—3, 50—2, 56—4,
57—4[etc.].

Date of publication: July 6, 1756 (*Daily Advertiser*).

Copies: Bodleian; British Library; Cambridge University Library;
*University of Chicago; *Cornell; etc. This work is found in
most major libraries.

Reviewed by Johnson in *LM*, I, no. IV (1756), 193—197; published
August 16, 1756 (*Daily Advertiser*; *Public Advertiser*).
Except for the first paragraph, Johnson's review is a reprint
of Article XXI, pp. 96—107 (with some slight omissions).

21. Johann Georg Keyssler, 1693—1743.
Title: TRAVELS / THROUGH / GERMANY, BOHEMIA,
HUNGARY, / SWITZERLAND, ITALY, and LORRAIN. /
Giving a TRUE and JUST / DESCRIPTION / OF THE /
PRESENT STATE of those COUNTRIES; / THEIR /
NATURAL, LITERARY, and POLITICAL HISTORY;
MANNERS, LAWS, / COMMERCE, MANUFACTURES,
PAINTING, SCULPTURE, ARCHITECTURE, / COINS,
ANTIQUITIES, CURIOSITIES of ART and NATURE, &c. /

ILLUSTRATED / With COPPER-PLATES, engraved from
Drawings taken on the Spot. / By JOHN GEORGE KEYSLER, /
Fellow of the ROYAL SOCIETY in LONDON. / Carefully
translated from the Second Edition of the GERMAN. / IN
FOUR VOLUMES. / VOL. I. / LONDON: / Printed for
A. LINDE, Bookseller to her Royal Highness the Princess
Dowager / of WALES, in *Catherine-street* in the *Strand*; and
T. FIELD, at the *Wheat-sheaf*, / the Corner of *Pater-Noster-Row*,
Cheapside. / MDCCLVI.

Volume I.

Collation: 4°: A⁴ a⁴ b² B—3U⁴

Contents: Page *i* title, *ii* blank, *iii—iv* Dedication, *v* vi—xiv Preface,
xv—xx Contents, *1* 2—503 text, *504* blank, 505—520 Index.
Pages 190, 191, 192 misnumbered 200, 201, 204; 252—
253 misnumbered 236—237; and in some copies (e.g.,
Cornell and Bodleian), 516 misnumbered 16. There are
four plates inserted: a frontispiece facing the title-page,
the others facing pages 47, 305 and 308.

Press figures: vi—2, viii—3, x—2 or none, *xix*—4, 2—2, 15—2,
20—3, 23—3, 28—3, 36—2, 42—3, 50—2, 71—2, 77—3,
79—2, 86—1, 95—3, 100—3, 108—1, 110—3, 117—1,
119—3, 122—3, 124—1, 130—2, 133—1, 138—2 or none,
144—3 or none, 146—3 or none, 148—2, 159—2, 160—3,
162—2, 165—3, 170—2, 172—3, 178—2, 184—3, 188—3
or none, 190 (misnumbered 200)—2 or none, 194—2,
200—2, 207—2, 208—3, 210—3, 216—2, 222—2, 228—3,
231—2, 234—2, 236—3, 244—3, 247—2, 250—3, 256—2,
258—3, 266—2 or none, 268—2, 274—3, 277—3, 286—2,
288—1, 293—2, 295—1, 298—3, 301—3, 306—1, 312—1,
314—3, 320—3, 322—2, 324—2, 330—2, 332—2, 343—1,
344—1, 350—1, 358—4, 360—4, 365—1, 367—1, 373—4,
375—4, 376—4, 378—2, 383—2, 384—3, 385—4, 390—2,
398—4, 400—3, 402—4, 404—4, 413—3, 423—3 or nonc,
424—3, 432—2, 434—3, 446—2, 453—3, 454—3, 456—3,
460—3, 463—3, 466—2, 477—4, 478—2, 484—3, 490—1,
496—1, 498—3, 509—1, 511—2. There are three press
figures in the 3B and 3M gatherings, but no signs of
cancellation. (Some copies also have P.F.3 on p. xii.)

Date of publication: On September 19, 1755 the *Daily
Advertiser* announced that "*Speedily will be publish'd,*

PROPOSALS *for printing*, by SUBSCRIPTION, A New
Collection of TRAVELS . . . by John George Keysler."
The proposals for printing in weekly numbers or in volumes
were published December 22, 1755 (*Daily Advertiser*).
Publication by numbers began in the first week of January,
1756, with each number containing three quarto sheets
(24 pages) which sold for 6d. In this first volume, the
number of each part is printed next to the signature in
gatherings B—2S (Numbers I—XIV); no gathering after
2S is marked as a "Numb." The first volume in quarto,
price in boards 12s., was published June 5, 1756 (*Public
Advertiser*). This is the only volume Johnson reviewed.
    The title-page of Vol. II is dated 1757. Vols III—IV
were published April 28, 1757 (*London Chronicle*,
April 26—28). A second edition of all four volumes in
quarto was advertised as published Nov. 22, 1757
(*London Chronicle*, Nov. 19—22).
    In 1757 there also appeared a rival translation of
Keyssler's *Travels*, in 4 vols., 12°, price bound 12s. The
editor was Godfrey Schutze and the publisher was J. Scott,
at the Black Swan in Pater-Noster-Row (see, e.g., the
Daily Advertiser of Dec. 27, 1757).

Copies: *Bodleian, *British Library (2 copies); *Cambridge
    University Library; *Cornell; Illinois; Yale; *D. D. Eddy.

Reviewed by Johnson in *LM*, I, no. V (1756), 240—247;
    published Sept. 15, 1756 (*Public Advertiser*). Johnson
    gives an abridgement of the life of Keyssler (*LM*, pp. 240—
    242; *Travels*, I, vi—xiii); he next quotes the first two para-
    graphs on page 153, then pages 156—159 (re. Patkul and
    Charles XII), then pages 99—102, 104—105 (re. the students
    at Tubingen).

22. Maximilien de Béthune, duc de Sully, 1559—1641.
Title: MEMOIRS / OF / MAXIMILIAN DE BETHUNE, / DUKE OF
    SULLY, / PRIME MINISTER TO / HENRY THE GREAT. /
    CONTAINING / The History of the LIFE and REIGN of that
    MONARCH, / And his own ADMINISTRATION under Him. /
    Translated from the FRENCH. / To which is added, / The Tryal
    of RAVAILLAC for the Murder of / HENRY the GREAT. /
    IN THREE VOLUMES. / VOL. I [II.] [III.] / LONDON, /
    Printed for A. MILLAR, in the Strand; R. and J. DODSLEY,

in Pall-Mall; / and W. SHROPSHIRE, in New-Bond-Street. / MDCCLVI.

The title-page of Vol. III lacks the semi-colon after "Pall Mall" in the third line from the bottom.

This is the first edition of the translation of Mrs. Charlotte Lennox.

Volume I.

Collation: 4°: A^4 a–c^4 a^4 B–3Y^4 3Z^2

Contents: A1^r half-title, A1^v blank, A2^r title, A2^v blank, A3^r–A4^r Dedication, dated Sept. 5, 1755 and signed Charlotte Lennox, A4^v blank, pages *i* ii–xxiv Preface, *xxv* xxvi–xxxii "A Summary . . .," *1* 2–58 *59* 60–110 *111* 112–157 *158* 159–204 *205* 206–257 *258* 259–320 *321* 322–375 *376* 377–426 *427* 428–472 *473* 474–540 text. Pages 164–165 misnumbered 165–164.

Press figures: A3^v–7, vi–8, x–8, xviii–7, xxxi–3, 4–3, 14–1, 22–5 [etc.].

Volume II.

Collation: 4°: A^2 a^4 B–4A^4 4B^2

Contents: A1^r half-title, A1^v blank, A2^r title, A2^v blank, pages *i* ii–viii "A Summary . . .," *1* 2–54 *55* 56–92 *93* 94–140 *141* 142–189 *190* 191–230 *231* 232–267 *268* 269–306 *307* 308–341 *342* 343–379 *380* 381–420 *421* 422–461 *462* 463–499 *500* 501–555 text, *556* blank. Page 116 is misnumbered as 166, 139 as 339, 172 as 170, 248 as 148, 498 as 506, 510 as 10.

Press figures: ii–9, iv–2, 6–9, 8–8, 13–8, 23–3, 30–1, 38–4 [etc.].

Volume III.

Collation: 4°: a^4 B–3X^4 3Y1

Contents: Page *i* title, *ii* blank, *iii* iv–vii "A Summary . . .," *viii* blank, *1* 2–48 *49* 50–107 *108* 109–165 *166* 167–231 *232* 233–275 *276* 277–317 *318* 319–356 *357* 358–377 text, *378* blank, *379* 380–407 text, *408* blank, 3G1^r–3Y1^v General Index. Page 112 is misnumbered as 111, 160 as 153, 192 as 190, 333 as 233; page 300 lacks number.

Press figures: vi—8, 7—9, 13—5, 20—6, 26—9 [etc.].

Date of publication: November 8, 1755 (*Public Advertiser; Whitehall Evening Post*, Nov. 6—8). In Sept. 1755 William Strahan printed 500 copies of this work (British Library Add. MSS 48803A, folio 14). Millar, Dodsley and Shropshire each owned a one-third share. Strahan printed 1000 copies of the octavo edition in March, 1757 (*Ibid.*, folio 22).

Copies: *Bodleian; *British Library; *Cambridge University Library; *Cornell; Kansas; Rochester; Yale; *D. D. Eddy.

Reviewed by Johnson in *LM*, I, no. VI (1756), 281—282; published October 15, 1756 (*Daily Advertiser; Public Advertiser*). Johnson quotes from Vol. I, 266—268.

23. Elizabeth Harrison

Title: MISCELLANIES / ON / Moral and Religious Subjects, / IN / PROSE and VERSE. / BY / ELIZABETH HARRISON. / [ornament] / [double rule] / LONDON: / Printed for the AUTHOR, / And Sold by J. BUCKLAND, at the Buck in Pater-noster Row; / and T. FIELD, at the Wheat-Sheaf in Cheapside. / MDCCLVI.

Collation: 8°: A⁸ a⁸ B—2B⁸

Contents: Page *i* title, *ii* blank, *iii*—iv Preface, *v—xxxii* list of sub-scribers, *1* 2—43 text, *44* blank, 45—220 *221* 222—238 *239* 240—352 *353* 354—380 text, *381* "Author to the Reader," *382* list of errata, *383—384* advertisements. Page 43 not numbered in some copies.

Press figures: *xi*—*, *xxvi*—1 or *, 2—*, 32—*, 47—*, 52—1 or *, 78—1 or *, 96—1 or *, 106—1 or *, 126—1, 142—1 or *, 158—1 or *, 174—1 or *, 190—1 or none, 208—*, 232—*, 249—*, 280—*, 302—1 or *, 308—1 or *, 326—1 or *, 344—1 or *, 354—1 or *, 378—1 or *. (See note, below.)

Date of publication: possibly October, 1756, since it was reviewed in the *Literary Magazine* of that month; however, it is most likely a pre-publication review in an effort to get more subscribers. See the *Public Advertiser*, Feb. 4, 1757, which describes the *Miscellanies* as "Just published and ready to be delivered to the Subscribers . . ." Price 5s. sewed in Pasteboard; some copies

available on fine paper, 10s. 6d. neatly bound and gilt. I have
found no earlier advertisements.

Copies: *Bodleian; *British Library; *University of Chicago;
Huntington; Illinois; *Yale.

Reviewed by Johnson in *LM*, I, no. VI (1756), 282—288, published
October 15, 1756 (*Daily Advertiser*). Johnson quotes a Reflection (pp. 77—79), three Letters (pp. 83—88, 97—104, 135—
138), and three Poems (pp. 254—255, 259, 274—278).

Note: As mentioned above, copies were printed on regular and on
fine paper. Apparently the Bodleian copy is on fine paper; it
measures 1½ inches thick exclusive of binding and end papers.
By the same measurement, however, the Illinois copy is only
⅞ inches thick, a regular paper copy. Initially I had hoped
that the different press figures, 1 or *, on the same pages
indicated whether the printing was done on regular or fine
paper. However, the hope was vain, for there is no relationship
between press figures and the quality (or thickness) of the
paper. All copies examined use 1 or * as press figures apparently
at random, and in my experience this book is unique in using
press figures in this manner. I have no idea why it was done.
    Two of the subscribers were "Mr. Hawkesworth, Author of
the Adventurer" and "Samuel Johnson, M.A."

24. Lewis Evans, 1700—1756.

Title: *Geographical, Historical, | Political, Philosophical and
Mechanical* | ESSAYS. | THE FIRST, CONTAINING | AN |
ANALYSIS | Of a GENERAL MAP of the | MIDDLE BRITISH
COLONIES | IN | *AMERICA;* | And of the COUNTRY of the
Confederate Indians: | A DESCRIPTION of the Face of the
Country; | The BOUNDARIES of the CONFEDERATES; |
AND THE | Maritime and Inland NAVIGATIONS of the several
RIVERS | and LAKES contained therein. | By *LEWIS EVANS.* |
The SECOND EDITION. | *PHILADELPHIA:* | Printed by
B. FRANKLIN, and D. HALL. MDCCLV. | And sold by J. and
R. DODSLEY, in *Pall-Mall*, LONDON.

Collation: 4°: π^2 A—D^4

Contents: Page *i* title, *ii* blank, iii—iv Preface, 1—32 text. Map
accompanies some copies.

60   The books Johnson reviewed

Press figures: none, although the rectos of the first two leaves of each
of the signed gatherings have a "2" on the same level as the
signature but not adjacent to it. Professor C. William Miller
informs me that these numbers were used to distinguish the
sheets of the second edition from the first; indeed, he states
that he has not encountered any press figures in his study of
Benjamin Franklin's printing.

References: Evans 7413; Miller 606a.

Date of publication: unknown, but probably this issue of the second
edition was published in London by the Dodsleys in January,
February or March, 1756. It was certainly later than the first
edition with the Dodsley imprint (Miller 605a) which was published in London October 22, 1755 (*Daily Advertiser*, Oct. 22;
Public Advertiser, Oct. 22; *London Evening-Post*, Oct. 21–23);
and presumably it was earlier than Evans' *Geographical, Historical and Mechanical Essays. Number II* . . . which was being
advertised by the Dodsleys in London late in March, 1756 ("In
a few Days will be publish'd . . ." *Public Advertiser*, March 26;
"This Day is publish'd . . ." *Daily Advertiser*, April 13).

Copies: In his *Benjamin Franklin's Philadelphia Printing*, 1728–
1766 . . . (Philadelphia: American Philosophical Society, 1974),
C. William Miller records the following copies (of 606a):
*British Library; Library of Congress (2 copies); Free Library
of Philadelphia; Library Company of Philadelphia; University
of Michigan (Clements); *New York Public Library; University
of Pennsylvania; Pennsylvania State Library, Harrisburg; Yale;
*Bodleian. In addition, there is a copy, with the colored map,
in *Cambridge University Library.

Reviewed by Johnson in *LM*, I, no. VI (1756), 293–299; published
October 15, 1756 (*Daily Advertiser*; *Public Advertiser*).
Johnson quotes from pages iii–iv, 3, 5–6, 15–16, 17–18,
31–32.

Note: In 1755 the Philadelphia firm of Franklin and Hall printed
two editions of the first of Lewis Evans' *Geographical* . . .
Essays, with the title-pages of both editions printed in two
states. This popular work, and the fine map which was meant to
accompany it, have been the subject of much scholarly investigation by Henry N. Stevens, Lawrence C. Wroth, Lawrence
Henry Gipson and others; but the most accurate concise
account is provided by C. William Miller in his bibliography of
Franklin imprints (nos. 605, 605a, 606, and 606a).

After so much has been written, only two points need discussion here: First, what is the textual relationship between
the two editions? Second, since Samuel Johnson reviewed the
work many months after both editions were available in
London, which edition did Johnson review?

In collating the two editions, one finds that both the inner
and outer formes of all gatherings are of different settings of
type, with many pages showing changes in lineation. Furthermore, it is clear that Evans revised and corrected the text of
the second edition fairly extensively: many footnotes and
marginal notes have been changed, added or deleted, and the
body of the text has also been revised – e.g., in the first
edition the last paragraph on page 24 reads, "The River thence
upward to the North Mountain is excellently fitted for large
Boats . . .," while in the second edition this is corrected to
read, "The River thence upward to an impassable Fall in the
South Mountain is excellently fitted for large Boats . . . ."
(Other changes are listed below.)

As the headnote of Johnson's review in the *Literary Magazine*
makes clear, Johnson reviewed a copy of the London issue
containing the Dodsley imprint – but of which edition? When
we examine the specific passages that Johnson quotes in his
review, we note (fortunately) that he is using passages which
incorporate textual changes. For example:

(1) In the first edition, page 3, the latitude of Oswego is
listed as "42:17" while in the second edition it is corrected to
"43:17."

(2) In the first edition, the last line of page 15 and the first
line of page 16 read, ". . . War with the French, amused . . .,"
which in the second edition is changed to ". . . War with the
French. Amused . . . ."

(3) In the first edition, page 31, lines 25–31 read: "It is
impossible to conceive, that had his Majesty been made
acquainted with its Value, the large Strides the French have
been making, for several Years past, in their Incroachments
on his Dominions; and the Measures still taken to keep the
Colonies disunited, and of impeding the generous Attempts of
his most zealous Subjects, his Majesty would have sacrificed,
to the Spleen of a few bitter Spirits, the best Gem in his Crown."
In the second edition this is changed to: "Had his Majesty been
made acquainted with its Value, the large Strides the French
have been making, for several Years past, in their Incroachments
on his Dominions; and the Measures still taken to keep the

Colonies disunited, and of impeding the generous Attempts of
his most zealous Subjects, it is impossible to conceive that
his Majesty would have sacrificed, to the Spleen of a few bitter
Spirits, the best Gem in his Crown."

(4) In the first edition, page 32, line 7 reads: ". . . Jealousy
of either's having the Superiority . . .," which in the second
edition is altered to, ". . . Jealousy of any one's having the
Superiority . . . ." Other examples could be cited in passages
quoted by Johnson, but these perhaps are the most readily
recognizable.

In each of these instances the text of the review in the
Literary Magazine uniformly follows the readings of the
second edition; hence, Johnson was using the second edition
with the Dodsley imprint (Evans 7413; Miller 606a).

Note: Donald J. Greene edits and reprints this review in the *Yale
Edition of the Works of Samuel Johnson* (New Haven and
London: Yale University Press, 1977), X, 197–212. In his
introduction, Greene states that "the text of [the *Literary
Magazine*] is followed here, though some clear errors of
transcription from Evans's volume have been corrected. These
are noted in the textual notes, together with other variants
from Evans's text, some of which suggest deliberate editing
(apparently for stylistic reasons), perhaps by Johnson himself"
(pp. 199–200). There are thirteen of these textual notes,
lettered a–m, found on pages 203–207, 209–210. One of them,
(d), is a textual conjecture by Greene. Three (b, e, and h)
consist of minor changes — the omission of one or two words
and a change in the use of italics — which are possibly "clear
errors of transcription" but may also reflect Johnson's tendency
to eliminate deliberately unnecessary words when copying
a text of this type. The remaining nine, however, involve
substantive changes which certainly "suggest deliberate
editing"; but as was mentioned above, these changes were made
by Evans in revising for the second edition, the text Johnson is
quoting in his review. (Some of the more important textual
changes between Evans' two editions are quoted above.)

One minor exception should be noted. In (k), Evans in the
first edition reads "in Ohio" and in the second edition, "on
Ohio"; the *Literary Magazine* reads "on the Ohio," a change
which could be either Johnsonian or compositorial.

There are other changes which Greene does not note, but
the results of collation remain the same: Johnson was reviewing
the revised second edition.

25. [Anonymous]

Title: A / LETTER / TO A / MEMBER of PARLIAMENT / In the
COUNTRY, / FROM / His FRIEND in LONDON, / Relative to
the CASE of / ADMIRAL BYNG: / WITH / Some original
PAPERS and LETTERS / Which passed during the Expedition. /
[rule] / *Audi alteram Partem.* / [double rule] / *LONDON:* /
Printed for J. COOKE, at the *King's-Arms*, in *Great- / Turnstile,
Holborn.* / [rule] / MDCCLVI. / [Price SIX-PENCE.]

Collation: 8°: A–B⁸

Contents: Page *1* half-title, *2* blank, *3* title, *4* blank, *5* 6–31 text,
32 blank.

Press figures: none.

There are two editions of this pamphlet, though not so identified on
their title-pages. One is a line-for-line reprint of the other, and no
press figures appear in either. They do, however, use different type
ornaments in three places: one edition, which I arbitrarily designate
A, uses a floral design both as the headpiece and as the decoration
of the initial letter "I" on page *5* and has an ornamental bust as the
tailpiece on page 31; in this edition page 12 ends "much greater Vio-".
  Edition B has an ornamental crest and two cornucopias as the
headpiece on page *5*; it has the ornamental "I" on the same page
within a square, black frame; the tailpiece on page 31 is a triangular
design composed of 28 identical type ornaments; and page 12 ends
"confess myself so uncourt-".
  Edition A seems much more common (all four copies in the British
Library, all three D. D. Eddy copies, etc.), but copies of B may be
found at Harvard and Cornell.
  These original editions sold for six pence, but Cooke also published
a cheap reprint which sold for three pence; it contains 16 pages,
excluding the title-page leaf, and is printed throughout with a smaller
font of type (copies: Cornell, Harvard, Yale).

Date of publication: October 2, 1756 (*Daily Advertiser; Public
Advertiser; London Evening-Post*). This is the date of the
first edition. However, in advertising the same work nine days
later, the *Public Advertiser* of Oct. 11, 1756 added this note:
"There has been so great a Demand for this Performance, that
some Booksellers could not possibly have the Number they
wanted, but there is this Day published another very large
Impression, so that the Public may now be supplied with any

Quantity." This explains the two editions (not impressions),
but it does not help to determine which is the earlier.

Copies: *Bodleian (3 copies); *British Library (4 copies); *Cambridge
    University Library; *Cornell; *Harvard (2 copies); Huntington;
    Illinois; Indiana; Kansas (2 copies) *Newberry Library; New
    York Public Library (2 copies); Pennsylvania State University;
    *Yale; Paul Latcham, Hereford; *D. D. Eddy (3 copies).

Reviewed by Johnson in *LM*, I, no. VI (1756), 299–309; published
    Oct. 15, 1756 (*Daily Advertiser; Public Advertiser*). Of the
    27 pages of text, Johnson quotes from pages 14–16, 18–19,
    22–23, 26–28. This is a double review: Johnson reviewed it
    with Shebbeare's *An Appeal to the People . . . Part the First*
    (London: J. Morgan), 1756 (see next item).

26. John Shebbeare, 1709–1788. [See note, below.]

Title: AN / APPEAL / TO THE / PEOPLE: / CONTAINING, / The
    Genuine and Entire LETTER of / Admiral *Byng* to the Secr. of
    the Ad–y: / OBSERVATIONS on those PARTS of it / which
    were omitted by the Writers of the *Gazette:* /AND / What
    might be the REASONS for such / OMISSIONS. / [quotation
    from Ovid] / PART the First. / *LONDON:* / Printed for
    J. Morgan, in *Pater-Noster-Row.* / 1756.

Collation: 8° (in 4's): A^2 B–K^4 L^2

Contents: $A1^r$ half-title, $A1^v$ blank, $A2^r$ title, $A2^v$ blank, pages
    1 2–76 text.

Press figures: none.

   The first state of page 76 contains no list of errata; the second
state lists 5 errata. (The British Library, Cambridge University
Library, Harvard, Yale and D. D. Eddy have copies of both states.)
I have seen no copy which corrects the errata. This first edition
sold for one shilling, but Morgan also published a cheap reprint
which sold for six pence: the Yale and D. D. Eddy copies contain
44 pages, including the title-page leaf, and are printed throughout
with a smaller font of type than the shilling editions.

Date of publication: October 7, 1756 (*Public Advertiser; London
    Evening-Post; General Evening Post*).

Copies: *Bodleian (4 copies); *British Library (5 copies);
    *Cambridge University Library (2 copies); *Cornell (2 copies);

*Harvard (Houghton; 2 copies); Huntington (2 copies); Indiana; Kansas; *Newberry Library; National Library of Scotland; Syracuse; *Yale; Paul Latcham, Hereford; *D. D. Eddy (5 copies).

Reviewed by Johnson in *LM*, I, no. VI (1756), 299–309; published Oct. 15, 1756 (*Daily Advertiser; Public Advertiser*). Johnson quotes from pages 16–23, 24–32, 60–61, 64–72. This is a double review; Johnson reviewed it with *A Letter to a Member of Parliament* . . . London: J. Cooke, 1756 (see preceding item).

Note: There are good reasons for attributing this piece to John Shebbeare. First, it is advertised in a list of nine works by Shebbeare on the last page of Shebbeare's *Fifth Letter to the People of England* (London: J. Morgan, 1757). Second, it is included in the remarkably detailed and accurate list of Shebbeare's writings at the end of his biography in the *European Magazine and London Review*, 14 (1788), 83–87, 166–168. The internal evidence is also strong, for the style and arguments match Shebbeare's known political writings of the period.

27. Jonas Hanway, 1712–1786.

Title: A / JOURNAL / OF / EIGHT DAYS JOURNEY / FROM / PORTSMOUTH to KINGSTON UPON THAMES; / through SOUTHAMPTON, WILTSHIRE, &c. / WITH / MISCELLANEOUS THOUGHTS, / MORAL and RELIGIOUS; / IN A SERIES OF SIXTY-FOUR LETTERS: / Addressed to two LADIES of the PARTIE. / To which is added, / AN ESSAY ON TEA, / Considered as pernicious to HEALTH, obstructing INDUSTRY, / and impoverishing the NATION: With an Account of its / GROWTH, and great CONSUMPTION in these KINGDOMS. / WITH / SEVERAL POLITICAL REFLECTIONS; / AND THOUGHTS ON PUBLIC LOVE. / IN TWENTY-FIVE LETTERS to the same LADIES. / [rule] / *By a GENTLEMAN of the Partie.* / [double rule] / *LONDON:* / Printed by H. WOODFALL, M.DCC.LVI.

Collation: $4°$: A^4 ($-$A4 [= 3A1?]) B–I^4 ($\pm$ I1) K–$2A^4$ ($\pm$ 2A4) $2B^4$ ($\pm$ 2B4) $2C^4$ ($\pm$ 2C2) 2D–$2I^4$ ($\pm$ 2I1) 2K–$2P^4$ ($\pm$ 2P2) 2Q–$2Z^4$ 3A1 (= A4?). X^2, the special title for the "Essay on Tea" and its list of Contents, is inserted between 2D1 and 2D2.

Contents: A1^r title, A1^v blank, A2^r–A3^r Contents, A3^v Errata, pages *1* 2–201 text of the sixty-four letters, *202* blank, X1^r

special title of "An Essay on Tea," X1^v blank, X2 Contents of the "Essay," 203—361 text of the "Essay," *362* blank.

Two plates are inserted: a frontispiece facing the volume title-page, and a frontispiece facing the special title of "An Essay on Tea."

Press figures: A2^r—1, A2^v—5, 5—3, 7—3, 12—3, 14—3, 20—5, 23—5, 27—4, 28—4, 36—2, 45—5, 46—3, 52—2, 54—2, 57—1, 61—2, 63—2, 70—3, 72—3, 74—3, 77—3, 82—3, 84—3, 93—3, 94—3, 102—2, 104—2, 109—2, 111—2, 114—3, 116—3, 124—2, 127—2, 135—2, 136—2, 140—4, 143—4, 149—2, 150—5, 156—4, 158—4, 162—2, 168—2, 170—2, 172—2, 178—5, 180—5, 183—2, 189—5, 190—2, 191—2, 198—5, 200—5, 205—4, 206—4, 208—4, 212—2, 214—5, 219—4, 224—4, 230—5, 232—4, 239—4, 240—4, 245—4, 254—2, 256—3, 258—2, 260—2, 270—5, 272—5, 274—3, 280—3, 284—1, 286—1, 291—5, 294—1, 296—1, 300—4, 303—4, 309—5, 311—5, 315—2, 316—2, 325—4, 327—4, 335—4, 336—4, 341—1, 342—1, 345—6, 350—6, 357—3, 358—3.

Note: The I, 2A, 2B, and 2P gatherings each have three press figures, but these are accounted for by a cancel with a press figure in each of those gatherings. The 2D gathering also has three press figures, but I can find no indication of cancellation.

Date of publication: probably February 28, 1756. Since the book was privately issued instead of being published, there are no advertisements in the newspapers. However, some copies are dated at the end of the last letter (p. 361) in an identical manner and in identical handwriting: "London 28 Feb: 1756." Copies so signed: Bodleian; Cambridge University Library; Cornell; Harvard (Houghton); Newberry Library; D. D. Eddy. In the second edition, that date is printed at the end of the text (II, 375).

Copies: *Bodleian; *Cambridge University Library; *Cornell; *Harvard (Houghton); *Hyde Collection (Somerville, N. J.); *Lewis Walpole Collection (Farmington, Conn.); *Newberry Library; *Yale; *D. D. Eddy.

Reviewed by Johnson in *LM*, I, no. VII (1756), 335—342, published November 15, 1756 (*Public Advertiser*). Johnson quotes from pp. 268—271 (Letter XIV), 285—298 (Letter XVII), and 301—307 (Letter XIX). In the second edition, 1757, these letters were revised and changed in number: Letter XIV became XV (II, 149—155), XVII became XVI (II, 158—178), and XIX was revised but retained its same number (II, 197–210).

28. Samuel Bever.

Title: THE / CADET. / A / MILITARY TREATISE. / [rule] / BY AN OFFICER. / [rule] / [quotation from Horace] / [rule] / [ornament] / [double rule] / *LONDON:* / Printed for W. JOHNSTON in *St. Paul's Church-yard.* / [rule] / MDCCLVI.

Collation: 8°: A⁸ (−A8) B–Q⁸ R²

Contents: Page *i* title, *ii* blank, *iii* iv–vi Dedication to the Duke of Cumberland, *vii* viii–x "To the Officers of the Army," *xi*–xii "Authors quoted in the following Collection," *xiii*–xiv Contents, *1* 2–244 text. Page 55 is misnumbered 35. A folding plate is inserted facing page 78.

Press figures: none.

Date of publication: October 9, 1756 (*Daily Advertiser; Public Advertiser;* and *General Evening Post*)

Copies: *British Library; *Cambridge University Library; Library of Congress; *Cornell (lacks folding plate); Huntington; *Newberry Library; *D. D. Eddy.

Reviewed by Johnson in *LM,* I, no. VII (1756), 343 [misnumbered 335]; published November 15, 1756 (*Public Advertiser*). Johnson quotes from pages 57–59, 111–113.

29. [Anonymous.]

Title: SOME / Further Particulars / IN / RELATION / TO THE / CASE / OF / Admiral BYNG. / FROM / ORIGINAL PAPERS, *&c.* / *Fiat Justitia!* / [rule] / By a GENTLEMAN of OXFORD. / [rule] / *LONDON:* / Printed for J. LACY, at the Corner of *St. Martin*'s Court, / *St. Martin*'s *Lane,* near *Leicester-Fields;* and are to be / sold at all the Pamphlet Shops and Booksellers in *London* / and *Westminster.* 1756. / [Price One Shilling.]

Collation: 8° (in 4's): *A*1 (= K4?) B–I⁴ K⁴ (−K4 = *A*1?)

Contents: *A*1ʳ title, *A*1ᵛ blank, pages 1–70 text.

Press figures: 12–1 or none, 23–1, 40–1, 48–2, 56–3, 58–1, 66–2.

Date of publication: October 27, 1756 (*Daily Advertiser; Public Advertiser*).

Copies: *Bodleian (3 copies); *British Library (3 copies); Harvard (Houghton); *Yale; Paul Latcham, Hereford; *D. D. Eddy (2 copies); *Cambridge University Library.

Reviewed by Johnson in *LM*, I, no. VII (1756), *344–48* (misnumbered 336–40); published November 15, 1756 (*Public Advertiser*). Johnson quotes from pages 4–12, 14–15, 17–20, 27–47.

Note: This pamphlet "may have been written by Paul Whitehead" (1710–1774); see Dudley Pope, *At 12 Mr Byng was shot . . .* (London: Weidenfeld and Nicolson, 1962), p. 322, n. 27.

30. David Mallet, 1705–1765. [See note 3, below.]

Title: THE / CONDUCT / OF THE / MINISTRY / Impartially Examined. / IN A / LETTER to the Merchants of LONDON. / [double rule] / LONDON: / Printed for S. BLADON, in Paternoster-Row. / MDCCLVI. / [Price One Shilling.]

Collation: 8°: A–D⁸ E²

Contents: Page *1* title, *2* blank, 3–68 text.

Press figures: 16–6, 20–8, 27–3, 45–7, 47–4, 63–8, 64–6.

Date of publication: October 30, 1756 (*Daily Advertiser; Public Advertiser; London Evening-Post*).

Copies: John Carter Brown; *Cambridge University Library (2 copies); *University of Chicago; *Cornell (2 copies); Harvard; Indiana; Kansas; New York Public Library (2 copies); *Yale (2 copies); *D. D. Eddy.

Reviewed by Johnson in *LM*, I, no. VII (1756), *348–350* 351 [pp. *348, 349, 350* misnumbered 340, 341, 342]; published November 15, 1756 (*Public Advertiser*). Johnson quotes from pages 9–19; he paraphrases and adapts pages 19, 25–35, 42, 52–53, 54, 55, 67.

Notes: 1. A second edition of the *Conduct of the Ministry* was published Nov. 11, 1756 (*Public Advertiser; General Evening Post*); copies of this edition are at John Carter Brown, Cornell (2 copies), Harvard, Illinois, and the collection of D. D. Eddy. It is barely possible that Johnson could have reviewed this edition, which was published four days before Johnson's review appeared in the *Literary Magazine*. However, textually the first and second editions are identical; in fact, they both have the same press figures and are the same impression of type throughout except for the title-page which was altered to "Second Edition" in the course of printing.

William Strahan printed 3,000 copies of this work — obviously including both the first and "second" editions — in October, 1756 (British Library Add. MSS 48800, folio 100).

2. Later an inexpensive reprint was issued under the same title (London: S. Bladon, 1756), but it contains 42 pages rather than 68; copies of it are at John Carter Brown, Harvard, and New York Public Library.

3. For confirmation of the attribution of authorship to David Mallet, see James A. Butler, "Samuel Johnson: Defender of Admiral Byng," *Cornell Library Journal*, no. 7 (Winter, 1969), pp. 25—47.

31. John Douglas, 1721—1807.

Title: BOWER [italic] AND TILLEMONT [italic] / COMPARED: / OR, / The first Volume of the pretended *original* and / *Protestant* HISTORY of THE POPES, shewn to / be chiefly a Traslation [sic] from a *Popish* one; / WITH / Some farther Particulars, relating to the True CHA- / RACTER and CONDUCT of the *Translator*. / TO WHICH WILL BE ADDED / A very circumstantial ACCOUNT of his Escape / From *Macerata* to *England*, as taken from his / own Mouth. / [rule] / By the AUTHOR of, *Six Letters from* A——d B——r *to Father* / Sheldon, *Provincial of the Jesuits, illustrated*, &c. / [rule] / [quotation from Virgil] / [double rule] / *LONDON,* / Printed for J. MORGAN in *Pater-noster-Row.* 1757 / [Price ONE Shilling and Six-pence.]

Collation: 8°: π1 A—F^8 G^6. D4^r not signed; D4^v signed D4.

Contents: π1^r title, π1^v blank, pages 1—106 text, *107* list of errata, *108* blank.

Press figures: none.

Date of publication: January 6, 1757 (*Public Advertiser; General Evening Post*, Jan. 4—6).

Copies: *Bodleian (2 copies); *British Library; *Cambridge University

Library; *Harvard (Houghton); Indiana (Lilly); *National
Library of Scotland; New York Public Library; Princeton; *Yale;
*D. D. Eddy. In addition to these copies which I have verified
personally, NUC lists the following: MHi; MnU; MiD; NBuG.

Reviewed by Johnson in *LM*, I, no. IX (Dec. 15, 1756 – Jan. 15,
1757), 442–453; published January 20, 1757 (*General Evening
Post*). Johnson quotes from pages 89–106. This is a double
review: Johnson reviewed it with Bower's *Answer to a Scurrilous
Pamphlet . . . Part I . . .* London: W. Sandby, 1757 (see next
item).

32. Archibald Bower, 1686–1766.

Title: MR. *BOWER's* / ANSWER / TO A / Scurrilous Pamphlet, /
INTITULED, / Six LETTERS from *A——d B——r* / TO / Father
Sheldon, Provincial of the Jesuits / in *England*, &c. / [rule] /
PART I. / [rule] / [quotation] / [double rule] / *LONDON:* /
Printed for W. SANDBY, at the *Ship*, opposite *St. Dunstan's* /
Church, *Fleet-Street.* / [rule] / M.DCC.LVII.

Collation: 8° (in 4's): π^2 A–Q^4 R^2

Contents: $\pi 1^r$ half-title, $\pi 1^v$ blank, $\pi 2^r$ title, $\pi 2^v$ blank, pages *1* 2–
127 text, 128–132 Appendix.

Press figures: 24–8, 31–3, 39–2, 47–4, 56–2, 58–2, 104–3, 118–
4, 128–3.

Date of publication: January 6, 1757 (*Daily Advertiser; Public
Advertiser; General Evening Post*, Jan. 4–6).

Copies: *Bodleian; British Library; *Cambridge University Library
(3 copies); *University of Chicago; Columbia; *Cornell;
Harvard; Huntington; *National Library of Scotland; New York
Public Library; Princeton; Texas; *Yale; *D. D. Eddy (2 copies).
In addition to these copies which I have verified personally,
NUC lists the following: NcD; MBAt; MnU; NBuG; ICN.

Reviewed by Johnson in *LM*, I, no. IX (Dec. 15, 1756 – Jan. 15,
1757), 442–453; published January 20, 1757 (*General Evening
Post*). Johnson quotes from pages 26–30 (with omissions); he
brilliantly paraphrases and condenses pages 30–41, 41–79,
99–112. This is a double review: Johnson reviewed it with
Douglas' *Bower and Tillemont compared . . .* London: J. Morgan,
1757 (see preceding item).

33. [Arthur Murphy, Henry Fox, *et al.*]

Title: THE / TEST. / A NEW / POLITICAL PAPER / IN THIRTY-SIX [*sic*] NUMBERS. / Founded on true WHIGGISH PRINCIPLES. / [rule] / [quotation] / [double rule] / LONDON, / Printed for S. HOOPER at Gay's Head, in the Strand. / MDCCLVIII. Note: This title-page and the entire periodical are reproduced as part of this series. The original title-page may be found in copies at Cornell and the Bodleian (Hope fol. 100).

Format: 2°. No pages are signed. There are six pages per issue. The thirty-five issues are dated from November 6, 1756 to July 9, 1757; I don't know why the volume title-page is dated 1758.

Contents: Pp. [2] title-page with verso blank, 1–6, 1–204 text, with the first page of each issue unnumbered. The first printing of the first issue contains no imprint, but the other thirty-four numbers (and the reprint of the first issue) show that they were printed in London for Samuel Hooper.

Press figures: 98–5, 100–8, 110–2, 116–5, 119–4, 122–4.

Copies: *Bodleian (2 copies); *British Library (2 copies); *Cambridge University Library; *Cornell; *Harvard (Houghton); *New York Public Library; *D. D. Eddy (incomplete).

Reviewed by Johnson in *LM*, I, no. IX (Dec. 15, 1756 – Jan. 15, 1757), 453–461; published January 20, 1757 (*General Evening Post*). Johnson quotes from the *Test*, numbers 1, 2 and 7 (dated respectively Nov. 6, Nov. 20 and Dec. 25, 1756). This is a double review; Johnson reviewed it with the *Con-Test* (see next item).

34. [Owen Ruffhead, Philip Francis, *et al.*]

Title: The Con-Test. (I have not located any volume title-page.)

Format: 2°: Page *1* signed B; no other pages signed. There are six pages per issue. The thirty-eight issues are dated from November 23, 1756 to August 6, 1757.

Contents: Pp. 1–228 text, with the first page of each issue unnumbered and pages 6 and 54 blank. The imprint of each number reads: "LONDON: Printed for C. CORBETT, opposite St. Dunstan's-Church, in Fleet-Street. Price 2*d*."

Press figures: none.

Copies: *Bodleian (2 copies); *British Library; *Cambridge University
   Library (lacks numbers 7 and 12); *University of Chicago;
   *Harvard (lacks number 9); Kansas; *New York Public Library
   (lacks number 19 and pp. 227–228); *Yale.

Reviewed by Johnson in *LM*, I, no. IX (Dec. 15, 1756 – Jan. 15,
   1757), 453–461; published January 20, 1757 (*General Evening
   Post*). Johnson quotes from the *Con-Test*, numbers 1, 2 and 7
   (dated respectively Nov. 23 and Nov. 30, 1756 and Jan. 1,
   1757). This is a double review; Johnson reviewed it with the
   Test (see preceding item).

35. William Whitehead, 1715–1785.

Title: ELEGIES. / WITH AN / ODE / TO THE / TIBER. / WRITTEN
   ABROAD. / By WILLIAM WHITEHEAD, Esq; / Register and
   Secretary to the Hon. Order of the BATH. / [Cut] / LONDON: /
   Printed for R. and J. DODSLEY in Pall-mall. 1757.

Collation: 4°: A^4 B–C^4

Contents: Page *1* half-title, *2* blank, *3* title, *4* blank, *5–22* text,
   23 advertisement, *24* blank.

Press figures: none.

Date of publication: February 4, 1757 (*Public Advertiser; General
   Evening Post; London Evening-Post*).

Copies: Bodleian; *British Library (3 copies); *Cambridge University
   Library; Harvard; *Cornell; *National Library of Scotland;
   Yale (2 copies); *D. D. Eddy.

Reviewed by Johnson in *LM*, II, no. X (1757), 31; published
   February 17, 1757 (*Daily Advertiser; General Evening Post;
   London Chronicle*). Johnson quotes from pages 10–11, 14, 6,
   16, 18.

36. [Anonymous]

Title: A / LETTER / TO A / Gentleman in the Country, / FROM /
   His Friend in LONDON: / Giving an / Authentick and
   circumstantial Account of / the Confinement, Behaviour, and
   Death of / ADMIRAL BYNG, / As attested by the Gentlemen
   who were present. / [rule] / *Mens conscia Recti.* / [double
   rule] / LONDON: / Printed for and sold by J. LACY, the

Corner of / St. Martin's-Court, St. Martin's-Lane, near / Leicester-Fields. MDCCLVII. / [Price One Shilling.]

Collation: 8° (in 4's): A^2 B—G^4

Contents: $A1^r$ blank, $A1^v$ Advertisement, $A2^r$ title, $A2^v$ blank, pages 1—48.

Press figures: 12—2, 24—1, 28—1, 36—1.

Date of publication: March 29, 1757 (*Daily Advertiser*).

Copies: *Bodleian (3 copies); *British Library (4 copies); *Cornell; Huntington; Kansas; *Yale; Paul Latcham, Hereford; *D. D. Eddy (2 copies).

Reviewed by Johnson in *LM*, II, no. XII (1757), 116—120; published April 16, 1757 (*Public Advertiser*). Johnson quotes from pages 6—13, 15—46.

37. Jonas Hanway, 1712—1786.

Title: A / JOURNAL / OF / EIGHT DAYS JOURNEY / FROM / PORTSMOUTH to KINGSTON UPON THAMES; / through SOUTHAMPTON, WILTSHIRE, &c. / WITH / MISCELLANEOUS THOUGHTS, / MORAL and RELIGIOUS; / IN SIXTY-FOUR LETTERS: / Addressed to two LADIES of the PARTIE. / To which is added / AN ESSAY ON TEA, / Considered as pernicious to HEALTH, obstructing INDUSTRY, / and impoverishing the NATION: With an Account of its / GROWTH, and great CONSUMPTION in these KINGDOMS. / With Several / POLITICAL REFLECTIONS; / AND / THOUGHTS on PUBLIC LOVE: / In Thirty-two LETTERS to two LADIES. / [rule] / In TWO VOLUMES. / [rule] / *By Mr. H*****.* / [rule] / *The Second Edition corrected and enlarged.* / [rule] / VOL. I. / [double rule] / *LONDON:* / Printed for H. WOODFALL in *Pater-noster-row,* and / C. HENDERSON under the *Royal Exchange.* / [rule] / MDCCLVII. Except for three small changes, the title-page of the second volume is identical.

Volume I.

Collation: 8°: π1 A^4 B—D^8 (± D4, unsigned; printed as Z4) E—O^8 (± O8, unsigned; printed as Z5) P—Z^8 (—Z4, 5 = D4 and O8). Z6 (as printed) signed Z4; see note, below.

Contents: $π1^r$ title, $π1^v$ blank, $A1^r$ half-title, $A1^v$ blank,

A2^r–A4^r Contents, A4^v blank, pages *1* 2–348 text. Page 237 misnumbered 257. A frontispiece is inserted facing the title-page.

Note: In the course of printing, Hanway found passages which offended him on pages 40 and 208. He therefore ordered the printer to cancel D4 (pp. 39–40) and O8 (pp. 207–208). The corrected texts of pages 39–40 and 207–208 were printed as unsigned leaves Z4, 5 between leaves signed Z3 and Z4. As indicated in the collation above, the two leaves numbered 39–40 and 207–208 with the corrected texts are cancels which were cut out of the Z gathering and substituted for the corresponding original leaves, while the Z gathering correctly has six leaves numbered 337–348 and with Z1–4 signed.

Press figures: A4^r–6, 10–4, 12–1, 26–3, 29–1, 38–4, 45–3, 63–4, 64–4, 77–4, 78–4, 89–3, 95–3, 104–3, 111–4, 123–3, 125–4, 137–1, 157–4, 159–2, 166–3, 169–3, 187–2, 189–3, 201–1, 207–4, 220–3, 223–3, 234–4, 237 (misnumbered 257)–4, 255–4, 256–4, 266–2, 269–2, 284–3, 286–3, 301–4, 302–4, 308–1, 319–2, 330–2, 344–2, 346–2.

Volume II.

Collation: 8°: π1 *A*^{4} B–2A^8 2B^4

Contents: π1^r title, π1^v blank, *A*1^r half-title, *A*1^v blank, *A*2^r–*A*4^r Contents, *A*4^v blank, pages 1–375 text. Page 364 misnumbered 264. A frontispiece faces the title page.

Press figures: 15–3, 32–2, 58–3, 68–2, 78–1.

Date of publication: April 27, 1757 ("Tomorrow will be published" . . . *Public Advertiser*, April 26; *London Evening-Post* and *Whitehall Evening Post*, April 23–26, 1757; "This Day is published" . . . *Public Advertiser*, April 27; *Whitehall Evening Post*, April 26–28, 1757). "Price bound 10s."

Copies: Copies as described in the collation and contents above, with D4 and O8 cancels and the Z gathering with six leaves, may be found in: *Bodleian; *British Library (290. c. 22–23); *Harvard (Houghton); Illinois; Kansas; and *Yale.
  However, *Cornell and *D. D. Eddy have copies, both

in original Jonas Hanway bindings, in which the sheets were bound as printed without any cancellation. These copies therefore collate simply π1 A⁴ B—Z⁸, but the pagination of the text is *1* 2—342, 39—40, 207—208, 343—348.

Reviewed by Johnson in *LM*, II, no. XIII (1757), *162* (misnumbered 161)—167, published May 17, 1757 (*Public Advertiser; London Chronicle; General Evening Post*). Johnson quotes from Vol. II, 30—31, 33—34, 37, 39—40, 46, 142—48 (all of Letter XIV), 161, 162, 184. Johnson quotes only from Vol. II, so his quotations are not affected by the cancels in Vol. I.

38. Soame Jenyns, 1704—1787.

Title: A / FREE INQUIRY / INTO THE / NATURE and ORIGIN / OF / EVIL. / In SIX LETTERS to -------. / [Engraving: the sun shining on the earth] / LONDON: / Printed for R. and J. DODSLEY in PALL-MALL. / MDCCLVII.

Collation: 8°: *A*² B—N⁸ *O*1. E4ʳ is missigned D4.

Contents: *A*1ʳ title, *A*1ᵛ blank, *A*2ʳ Contents, *A*2ᵛ blank, pages *1* 2—21 text of Letter I, *22* blank, *23* special title for Letter II, *24* blank, *25* 26—41 text, *42* blank, *43* special title for Letter III, *44* blank, *45* 46—78 text, *79* special title for Letter IV, *80* blank, *81* 82—101 *102* 103—120 text, *121* special title for Letter V, *122* blank, *123* 124—150 text, *151* special title for Letter VI, *152* blank, *153* 154—193 text, *194* blank. Page 102 is not numbered, and page 157 is misnumbered 517.

Press figures: 2—1, 15—1, 26—1, 34—1, 50—6, 52—8, 72—1, 96—5, *102*—7, 116—2, 127—3, 142—8, 154—5, 171—7 or none, 178—8.

Date of publication: March 30, 1757 (*Public Advertiser*). William Strahan printed 750 copies of this first edition in March, 1757 (British Library Add. MSS 48800, folio 83).

Copies: *Bodleian; *British Library; *Cambridge University Library; Kansas; *Michigan State University; *Pembroke College, Cambridge (L.S. 324. 628); *Queens' College, Cambridge (P. 323¹); *John R. B. Brett-Smith, Princeton, N.J.; *D. D. Eddy.

Reviewed by Johnson in *LM*, II, no. XIII (1757), 171—175, published
   May 17, 1757 (*Public Advertiser; London Chronicle; General
   Evening Post*); and in *LM*, II, no. XIV (1757), 251—253, published June 17, 1757 (*Public Advertiser*); and in *LM*, II, no. XV
   (1757), *299—304* (misnumbered 301—306), published July 19,
   1757 (*Public Advertiser*). Johnson quotes from pages 3, 5, 13,
   14—15, 18, 26, 27—28, 28—30, 33—35, 36—37, 40, 47—48,
   49—50, 50—52, 54—56, 56—58, 67—68, 83—95, 98—99, 145,
   149—50 (thus quoting from 50 of 181 pages of text).

The Second Edition: published May 31, 1757 (*Daily Advertiser;
   Public Advertiser*). Strahan's ledgers indicate that he printed
   750 copies of the second edition in May, 1757 (British Library
   Add. MSS 48800, folio 83).

Collation: 8°: A^4 (−A4 = *O*1) B—N^8 *O*1 (= *A*4)

Contents: *A*1^r half-title "A / FREE INQUIRY / INTO THE /
   NATURE and ORIGIN / OF / EVIL. / THE SECOND EDITION."
   *A*1^v blank, *A*2^r title (same as first edition), *A*2^v blank, *A*3^r
   contents, *A*3^v blank, pages *1* 2—21 [etc.] same as the first
   edition, except that page 102 is numbered and page 157 is
   correctly numbered.

Press figures: 2—1, 4—3, 29—7, 38—3, 50—3, 56—2, 74—8, 93—2,
   107—8, *123*—1, 139—3, 158—1, 173—3, 174—2. (Some copies
   "lack" the press figure on page 173 because they have been
   trimmed; the press figure is one inch below the last line of the
   text.)

Copies: *University of Chicago; *Cornell (2 copies); Illinois;
   *Yale (2 copies); *D. D. Eddy.
       One Cornell copy, one Yale copy, and the Chicago copy
   lack the half-title.

Note: There has been considerable confusion in differentiating the
   first two editions of this work, for a copy of the second
   edition which lacks the half-title — as do three of the copies
   examined — is identical with the first edition in title-page,
   collation, and contents. The editions may be distinguished in
   several ways:
       (1) They have different press figures.
       (2) In the first edition, page 102 is not numbered, while in
            the second it is.
       (3) In the first edition, page 157 is misnumbered 517, while
            in the second it is numbered correctly.

(4) In the first edition, E4ʳ is missigned D4, while in the second it is signed correctly.

(5) In the first edition, page 64, line 15 reads: "in chains stuck round with pointed nails." In the second and all subsequent editions, "chains" is corrected to "chairs."

"The THIRD EDITION, amended" London: R. and J. Dodsley, 1758 was published April 20, 1758 (*Public Advertiser; Whitehall Evening Post*). Strahan printed 500 copies of the third edition in April, 1758 (British Library Add. MSS 48800, folio 83).

Collation: A^2 B–N⁸ O^2

Contents: $A1^r$ title, $A1^v$ blank, $A2^r$ Contents, $A2^v$ blank, pages *1* 2– 22 text, *23* special title, *24* blank, *25* 26–41 text, *42* blank, *43* special title, *44* blank, *45* 46–77 text, *78* blank, *79* special title, *80* blank, *81* 82–123 text, *124* blank, *125* special title, *126* blank, *127* 128–153 text, *154* blank, *155* special title, *156* blank, *157* 158–195 text, *196* blank.

Press figures: 16–5, 29–7, 30–5, 34–3, 62–4, 72–6, 93–8, 109– 6, 114–1, 138–4, 141–2, 146–3, 173–8, 185–6, 190–8.

Copies: *Bodleian; *British Library; Harvard; *University of Michigan; *Syracuse University; *D. D. Eddy.

The FOURTH EDITION, with an additional Preface, and some explanatory Notes. London: R. and J. Dodsley, 1761. Strahan printed 500 copies of the fourth edition in June, 1761 (British Library Add. MSS 48800, folio 83).

Collation: A^2 (= Q7, 8) B–P⁸ Q⁸ (–Q7, 8 [= A^2])

Contents: $A1^r$ title, $A1^v$ blank, $A2^r$ Contents, $A2^v$ blank, pages *i* ii–xxx Preface, *31* special title, *32* blank, *33* 34–53 text, *54* blank, *55* special title, *56* blank, *57* 58–72 text, *73* special title, *74* blank, *75* 76–106 text, *107* special title, *108* blank, *109* 110–155 (misnumbered 551) text, *156* blank, *157* special title, *158* blank, *159* 160–189 text, *190* blank, *191* special title, *192* blank, *193* 194–236 text. Page 155 misnumbered 551.

Press figures: xiv–1, xxvii–3, 46–8, 50–5, 61–1, 66–5, 68–6, 96–8, 102–4, 112–1, 114–4, 134–4, *159*–1, 185–4, 206–2, 219–6, 220–5, 233–2, 235–4.

Copies: Bodleian; British Library; *Harvard (Houghton Library, in a Thomas Hollis binding).

Note: Also in 1761, the Dodsleys published Soame Jenyns'
Miscellaneous Pieces, in Two Volumes, the second volume of
which contains Jenyns' *Free Inquiry*, again listed as the "Fourth
Edition" and having the same contents and pagination (except
that page 155 is correctly numbered). However, collation of
these two "fourth" editions of 1761 indicate that they are of
different settings of type and both have completely different
sets of press figures. Subsequent editions of the *Miscellaneous
Pieces* also reprint the *Free Inquiry*.

The FIFTH EDITION, with an additional Preface, and some explanatory Notes. London: Printed for J. Dodsley in Pall-Mall, 1773.

Copies: Bodleian; British Library; Cambridge University Library;
D. D. Eddy.

Note: Listed above, in an increasingly degressive manner, are the
five separate editions of the *Free Inquiry* published in London
during Jenyns' lifetime. Johnson reviewed only the first edition;
but since it is Johnson's most famous and widely reprinted
review, I have attempted to make clear some of the relationships
and differences in the editions.

39. Jonas Hanway, 1712–1786.

A Paper in the *Gazetteer* of May 26, 1757.

Copies examined: none. Apparently no copy of the *Gazetteer* of this
date is in existence. Mr. Robert Haig informs me that he has
searched the files of the British Library diligently but with no
success. Queries to other libraries have been equally futile.
A query in the *Johnsonian News Letter* brought no response.

Answered by Johnson in *LM*, II, no. XIV (1757), 253–56 (misnumbered 356), published June 17, 1757 (*Public Advertiser*).

CHAPTER III

JOHNSON'S TECHNIQUES
AS A REVIEWER

A discussion of Johnson's reviews necessarily involves related topics, such as the factors that influenced Johnson's choice of books and the general problem of the distribution of books for review in the mid-eighteenth century. So little is known about book distribution that one is faced with many questions: for example, were books sent gratis by publishers to leading periodicals and critics? Were the books sent before or after the official date of publication? Was there any connection between book publishers and review periodicals? Perhaps a few tentative answers may be suggested.

Presumably publishers sent free copies of books to periodicals for review. It was the customary practice for an author to sell the copyright of a work to a publisher even before the book was printed;[1] it was to the publisher's financial advantage, therefore, to see that the book was advertised and reviewed. Of course, if an author knew a reviewer personally (as Charlotte Lennox knew Johnson), or if the author had a financial interest in the book, or if he were eager for fame and publicity, then he might very well take the initiative in trying to get his book reviewed.

The majority of reviews were completely anonymous; some were signed with initials or pseudonyms, but this was not the usual practice.[2] If, therefore, a publisher wanted to have a new book reviewed in the *Monthly Review* or the *Critical Review*, in most instances he probably had little choice but to send the book to the editorial office of the periodical. Although evidence is lacking, we may perhaps assume that the normal procedure was for the editor to receive the books, to decide which ones should be reviewed, and then to assign (or offer) them to the particular writers who worked for him. As is the case with some modern journals, a reviewer often did not know the identity of other reviewers on the staff of the same periodical.[3]

I believe we may also assume that no periodicals were forced to buy the books they reviewed; surely the *Monthly Review* and the *Critical Review* would not have remained in business long, or at least they would have reviewed fewer books. It is also reasonable to suppose that reviewers — then as now — were allowed to keep the books they reviewed. One cannot imagine that the offices of any periodical would wish to keep all review copies, and surely the publishers would not have much success if they demanded them back. If this were the custom, then one wonders in Johnson's case, at least, what he did with his review copies. Of the thirty-nine items he reviewed in the *Literary Magazine*, only two —Mrs. Lennox' translation of Sully's *Memoirs* and the first volume of Birch's *History of the Royal Society* — are listed in the sale catalogue of Johnson's library.[4] Moreover, since the authors were Johnson's friends, these two items may have been gifts.

As a general rule, no book was reviewed before its official date of publication; in fact, it is quite possible that normally no book was even sent to a reviewer until it was published. Naturally there were exceptions. For example, Johnson's edition of Shakespeare was reviewed in the October 10, 1765 issue of the *St. James's Chronicle* on the very day it was published because, the reviewer stated, ". . . as we obtained a Sight of the Editor's valuable Preface a few Days ago, we shall now oblige our Readers with Extracts from it, together with some Remarks . . . ." Of all the items in the *Literary Magazine*, apparently the only one which Johnson reviewed before it was published was Elizabeth Harrison's *Miscellanies*. Johnson reviewed it in October, 1756, but apparently it was not delivered to the subscribers until February, 1757 (see Chapter II, item no. 23). In his review Johnson says that ". . . this collection which perhaps being published only for the subscribers, will not be generally read . . . ." He praises the book very highly for being written by those ". . . who please and do not corrupt, who instruct and do not weary . . .," and he praises Elizabeth Harrison for her "modesty and piety."[5] Johnson, therefore, probably reviewed the book when he did to encourage more people to subscribe to it. Such cases are genuine exceptions, however, and do not invalidate the general rule.[6]

Assuming, then, that publishers sent review copies of books, soon after they were published, to the offices of the *Literary Magazine*, and assuming that these copies were left to Johnson's disposal and discretion,[7] what were the factors, we may ask, that influenced Johnson's choice of books for review?

Even though Johnson was working for a group of men that included printers and publishers, there is no indication that he favored their books in choosing those to be reviewed. If anything, he seems to have avoided their books, for only two of the thirty-nine items reviewed are associated with members of the "syndicate": Faden was the printer of Murphy's *Gray's-Inn Journal*, and Payne was the publisher of Johnson's edition of Browne's *Christian Morals*. Dodsley's name is found on six imprints, Millar's is on four, and those of Morgan, Sandby, and Davis and Reymers are each found three times. Conspicuous by their absence are the names of Wilkie and Newbery. Johnson, therefore, apparently did not choose his books on the basis of their printers or publishers.

Johnson surely reviewed some books because he had a personal involvement in them — e.g., he may have subscribed to the book, or he may have edited it, or he may have contributed a biographical introduction, a preface, or a dedication to it. He prefixed the life of Sir Thomas Browne to his well edited and annotated edition of *Christian Morals*. He may have subscribed to Harrison's *Miscellanies*, considering her a worthy subject of charity. He may also have written the Preface to Hampton's translation of the *History of Polybius*.[8] He certainly wrote the Dedication to Mrs. Lennox' translation of Sully's *Memoirs* and — as we saw in Chapter I — he reviewed it in the *Literary Magazine* for the sake of friendship. He probably reviewed other works because he knew and liked the authors — e.g., Birch's *History of the Royal Society*, Warton's *Essay on Pope*, and Murphy's *Gray's-Inn Journal*. He may have reviewed the four Bower pieces because he knew and respected John Douglas and William Faden, both of whom were involved in the controversy. However, one must not push such suppositions too far. At this time he had other friends who wrote books, and he also subscribed to other works, but he did not review them. For example, he knew John Baskerville[9] and subscribed to his handsome quarto edition of Virgil (1757), but he did not review it. He was a very good friend of Elizabeth Carter and subscribed to her quarto edition of *Epictetus* (1758), but, so far as is known, he did not review it in any periodical. Also, he wrote the Dedication for Payne's *Game of Draughts* (1756), the Preface to Rolt's *Dictionary of Trade and Commerce* (1756), and the first paragraph of the Preface for Baretti's *Italian Library* (1757),[10] but he did not review them. Therefore, friendship for an author and personal involvement in a book were clearly not always — or even regularly — the predominant factors in Johnson's choice of books to review. Moreover, since those factors are not applicable (so far as is known) to the majority of the books reviewed in the *Literary Magazine*, one is left with the probability that Johnson simply chose most of the books because he was interested in their contents.

However, that is a point which is neither so obvious nor so true as it might seem initially. For example, it is reasonable to suppose that the books in the library of such a man as Johnson would reflect his genuine interests. If, therefore, one examines the books listed in the sale catalogue of Johnson's library, one discovers many interests in addition to those exhibited by his reviews in the *Literary Magazine*. The library reflects a very serious interest in the Greek and Roman classics; none are reviewed in the *Magazine* except Hampton's *History of Polybius*, which is in English translation. The library contained many volumes in the fields of law and of French literature, two areas which are totally neglected by the magazine. Johnson owned many volumes of sermons and other religious works, yet he reviewed no sermons and only a few religious (or moral or philosophical) books.

However, merely because the reviews in the magazine do not reflect all of Johnson's interests, one must not infer his lack of interest in the books he chose to review. Johnson's love of tea, for example, would scarcely be reflected by books in his library, yet no one who knew Johnson ever questioned his devotion to the beverage. Johnson, after all, was writing for a general magazine which was trying to be popular, and it was his duty to select books for review which would appeal to the tastes of his readers. Within such limitations, he undoubtedly selected books which he too found interesting.

Thirteen of the thirty-nine items reviewed deal with politics and current events: six concern Minorca and Admiral Byng (nos. 1, 25, 26, 29, 30, 36); three others discuss aspects of contemporary politics (nos. 24, 33, 34); and four are concerned with the Archibald Bower controversy (nos. 11, 12, 31, 32). Nine reviews pertain to natural history and other scientific topics (nos. 2, 3, 8, 10, 13, 15, 16, 18, 20); they range from natural histories of Jamaica, Aleppo and the Scilly Islands to a history of the Royal Society, as well as instructions for making bee boxes and for bleaching linen. Five reviews are of books dealing with some aspect of religion, morals, or philosophy (nos. 9, 14, 17, 23, 38). Only three reviews are of literary works: Murphy's *Gray's-Inn Journal* (no. 4), Warton's *Essay on Pope* (no. 5), and Whitehead's *Elegies* (no. 35). The remaining books may be classified under such headings as history, travel, military matters, classics, and tea.

It is not really surprising to find Johnson reviewing any of these books, but we cannot help wondering why he reviewed so few literary and philosophical works. In the early months of 1757, when he was still working for the magazine, he assigned to others (especially to Arthur Murphy) such books as Dyer's *The Fleece*, Home's *Douglas*, Francklin's *Translation, a Poem*, David Hume's *Four Dissertations*, the periodical the *Connoisseur*, and Burke's *Sublime and Beautiful*. One

cannot help believing that Johnson must have been interested in some
of these, especially Hume and Burke. Why he did not review them
remains a puzzle.

* * * * *

It is difficult to make valid generalizations concerning the book
reviews of Johnson's time; but perhaps it is safe to say that most
eighteenth-century reviewers for English periodicals saw their task
as presenting an accurate summary of the contents of the book plus
their own critical commentary. As a result the eighteenth-century
reviewer used many more extracts (direct quotations, paraphrases,
and skillful condensations) than does his modern counterpart.
Although any piece of writing reflects the author's intelligence,
experience, and critical faculties, Johnson also used those abilities
in selecting and preparing the extracts he used so extensively in his
reviews.

In discussing Johnson's techniques as a reviewer, one must
differentiate the various types of extracts that he made. Boswell's
failure to make such a distinction is shown in the following passage
from the *Life:*

> I mentioned the very liberal payment which had been
> received for reviewing; and, as evidence of this, that it had
> been proved in a trial, that Dr. Shebbeare had received
> six guineas a sheet for that kind of literary labour.
> JOHNSON, 'Sir, he might get six guineas for a particular
> sheet, but not *communibus sheetibus.*' BOSWELL. 'Pray,
> Sir, by a sheet of review is it meant that it shall be all of
> the writer's own composition? or are extracts, made from
> the book reviewed, deducted?' JOHNSON. 'No, Sir: it is
> a sheet, no matter of what.' BOSWELL. 'I think that it is
> not reasonable.' JOHNSON. 'Yes, Sir, it is. A man will more
> easily write a sheet all his own, than read an octavo volume
> to get extracts.' To one of Johnson's wonderful fertility of
> mind, I believe writing was really easier than reading and
> extracting; but with ordinary men the case is very different.
> A great deal, indeed, will depend upon the care and judge-
> ment with which the extracts are made. I can suppose the
> operation to be tedious and difficult: but in many instances
> we must observe crude morsels cut out of books as if at
> random; and when a large extract is made from one place,
> it surely may be done with very little trouble. One, however,
> I must acknowledge, might be led, from the practice of

> reviewers, to suppose that they take a pleasure in original
> writing; for we often find that, instead of giving an accurate
> account of what has been done by the authour whose work
> they are reviewing, which is surely the proper business of
> a literary journal, they produce some plausible and ingenious
> conceits of their own, upon the topicks which have been
> discussed.[11]

Here Boswell is making a normal assumption: that the process of
making extracts was a simple one, and that it may have involved
no more for the reviewer than marking passages in the book to serve
as copy for the compositor, or (at most) transcribing the passages to
be used.

   Johnson surely used this method in writing many of his reviews.
As we have seen in Chapter I, when he offered to review Mrs. Lennox'
translation of Sully's *Memoirs*, he asked her to "point me out a passage that can be refered to the present times," and so in this instance
he presumably did not even choose the extract. In many instances he
merely chose extracts which seemed to be representative of the work.
In the case of periodical essays, for example, he merely prints extracts
from the first, second, and seventh issues of both *The Test* and *The
Con-Test* (nos. 33, 34), and he prints all of essay no. 93 from the
duodecimo edition of Murphy's *Gray's-Inn Journal* (no. 4). He did
the same thing in reviewing scientific books composed of many
different sections covering a wide variety of topics. From Birch's
History of the Royal Society (no. 3), he quotes Dr. Needham's
article on varnish (Birch, I, 51–52) and Mr. Grey's article on
Greenland (Birch, I, 199–202); from Browne's *Civil and Natural
History of Jamaica* (no. 18), Johnson gives a number of verbatim
extracts which are fairly evenly divided between the two sections
on flora and fauna and seem to be representative of each; from the
Philosophical Transactions of the Royal Society, Vol. XLIX, Pt. I,
for 1755 (no. 20), he reprints all of Article XXI, with a few slight
omissions, concerning various aspects of Turkey. Stephen Hales's
An Account of a useful Discovery . . . (no. 15) is composed of
three articles which later were published in the *Philosophical Transactions*, and Johnson gives a good account by printing representative
extracts from all three.

   In fact, so many of the books Johnson selected are composed of
miscellaneous articles discussing various subjects that it would seem
natural (and almost inevitable) to review them by giving extracts.
Where there is no continuity, plot, development, or unity, one
cannot very well present a concise summary. From Harrison's
Miscellanies (no. 23), for example, Johnson reprints a "Reflection,"

three letters, and three poems. The first edition of Hanway's *Journal* (no. 27) is composed of "Miscellaneous Thoughts, Moral and Religious, in a Series of Sixty-four Letters . . . to which is added, An Essay on Tea . . . in Twenty-five Letters"; Johnson reviews the section on tea by giving large extracts from Letters XIV, XVII, and XIX. He gives a fair sample of Samuel Bever's varied military essays, *The Cadet* (no. 28), by quoting two passages from pages 57–59 and 111–13. Of Robert Keith's book (no. 17), Johnson says accurately: "This catalogue consisting almost merely of names and dates, does not easily admit of an extract" (*LM*, I, 171); the review consists of one extract from a biography of bishop Robert Leighton (Keith, pp. 158–60) and the reprint of a letter concerning the Revolution of 1688 (Keith, pp. 41–45). Books of travel necessarily present many of the same difficulties; so in reviewing Keyssler's *Travels through Germany* (no. 21), Johnson gives an abridgement of the life of Keyssler and then quotes several isolated incidents from his travels.

Johnson's skill in making extracts is such that he occasionally almost misleads the reader by making a dull or inconsequential pamphlet seem interesting. For example, Parkin's *Account of the Invasion under William Duke of Normandy* (no. 19) is a foolish, dull piece which Johnson summarizes accurately in the first sentence of his review: "This pamphlet is published to prove what nobody will deny, that we shall be less happy if we were conquered by the *French*" (*LM*, I, 186). However, he then proceeds to quote (from pp. 30–34) the one passage of historical interest in the pamphlet (in which Parkin refutes the claims of Sir Henry Spilman concerning the right to certain lands in Norfolk), and so he tends to make the pamphlet seem better than it is.

Another example is the review of Lewis Evans' map and essay (no. 24). Johnson admits that "as this treatise consists principally of descriptions of roads disfigured by Indian names, and of authorities on which the map depends, it scarcely admits of extract or epitome. There are however interspersed some observations like green spots among barren mountains from which our readers will obtain a just idea of the situation and state of those untravelled countries" (*LM*, I, 295). By presenting Evans' general account of the map (Preface, pp. iii–iv) and by concentrating on the few political passages (especially pp. 15–16 and 31–32) in the work, Johnson again produces a fascinating and well-written account which, however, does not accurately reflect the total contents of the work.

Johnson also defended the uniform payment for all parts of a review because many of his "extracts" are actually skillful condensations which necessitate careful reading and a good understanding of the book being reviewed; they also require a good writer. Examples of the process are plentiful. For instance, in his *Natural History of Aleppo* (no. 8), Alexander Russell discusses the dromedary:

> The dromedary, by all I could ever discover, is nothing but a high breed of the *Arab* camel. The only distinction observed is, that it is of a lighter and handsomer make; and, instead of the solemn walk to which the others are accustomed, it paces, and is generally esteemed to go as far in one day as the others do in three [p. 57].

Johnson merely says: "The *Dromedary* seems the most elegant sort of the *Arab Camel*, and perhaps differs from him only as a race-horse from a cart-horse" (*LM*, I, 80); the closing comparison is Johnson's contribution.

The following passage is from Thomas Blackwell's *Memoirs of the Court of Augustus*, Vol. II (no. 7):

> BUT, a little before the News of this public Ruin could reach *M. Brutus*, his Patience was put to the highest trial by a private Calamity. He had been married, early in Life, to *Clodia*, a Daughter of *Appius Claudius Pulcher*, and Niece of the flagitious Tribune. *Cn. Pompey*'s eldest Son, by marrying her younger Sister, was become his Brother-in-law: but, whether the Manners of the Family to which he was then allied did not please him, or whether he had reason to be dissatisfied with the Lady's Behaviour during his Absence; it is certain, that, soon after his Return from the Government of the nearer *Gaul*, he entertained Thoughts of a Separation. This raised a good deal of Talk while it continued in suspence; and the Women of the *Clodian* Family, as might be expected on such occasions, did not fail to inveigh bitterly against BRUTUS; ... [Blackwell, II, 3].

Johnson condenses this passage in his review, and the result is printed within quotation marks. It reads:

> 'About this time *Brutus* had his patience put to the *highest* trial: he had been married to *Clodia*; but whether the family did not please him, or whether he was dissatisfied with the lady's behaviour, during his absence; he soon entertained thoughts of a separation. *This raised a good deal of talk*, and the women of the *Clodian* family inveighed bitterly against *Brutus* ...' [*LM*, I, 42].

Some Further Particulars in Relation to the Case of Admiral Byng (no. 29) was published Oct. 27, 1756, and in reviewing it the next month Johnson says, ". . . We shall make a faithful extract from this pamphlet . . ." (*LM*, I, *344* —misnumbered 336). One passage he "epitomizes" is the following:

> And now *April* the first at ten in the Morning, the Admiral received by an Express a Letter from the Secretary of the Admiralty, together with his Instructions, dated *March* the 30th, inclos'd, which the same Secretary had on the 21st of the Month preceding prepar'd him to expect on the 23d following: The Letter required him, in the Name of the Board, to put to Sea with the first fair Wind, and to proceed without Loss of Time to the *Mediterranean* . . . [pp. 8–9].

In Johnson's "faithful extract" the passage reads:

> *April* the first the Admiral received a letter, that required him to proceed without loss of time to the *Mediterranean* [*LM*, I, *344*].

This passage is a fair example of Johnson's skill in "epitomizing." The eighty-two words of the original passage are contracted to twenty; all of them, except "that," are in the original and are presented in exactly the same order as the original; yet the full substantive meaning of the passage is preserved.

In some reviews Johnson condenses and paraphrases even more rigorously. His review of Stephen White's *Collateral Bee-Boxes* (no. 2) is a fair example. The first paragraph quotes from White's introduction; paragraph 2 accurately summarizes Chapter I (pp. 13–20); paragraph 3, Chapters II and III (pp. 20–30); paragraph 4, Chapter IV (pp. 30–33); paragraph 5, Chapter V (pp. 34–41); paragraphs 6–8, Chapter VI (pp. 41–52); and paragraph 9 summarizes, within quotation marks, pages 57–62. Thus, in slightly more than one page of the *Literary Magazine*, Johnson accurately summarizes an entire pamphlet.

Although only a few samples of this practice are shown, Johnson uses it extensively. Indeed, it seems to be his most distinctive single technique as a book reviewer. Johnson's "extracts" are generally much better written than the books he is quoting from, and it is amazing to see how successful he is in conveying an author's thoughts and information in so many fewer words than the originals. His ruthless excisions of unnecessary words and phrases reminds one of an editor's revising an excessively long manuscript. As one who has spent years working with the books that Johnson reviewed, I have

wished on numerous occasions that a man of Johnson's abilities had
been employed to edit the manuscripts of those books before they
were printed.[1][2]

Another procedure which Johnson uses in a few reviews is to go
systematically through the entire book, condensing, paraphrasing,
and quoting material from almost every page. Excluding pamphlets,
there are at least three fine examples of this: his reviews of Joseph
Warton's *Essay on Pope*, Vol. I (no. 5); William Borlase' *Observations
on the Islands of Scilly* (no. 10); and Soame Jenyns' *A Free Inquiry
into the Nature and Origin of Evil* (no. 38).

Johnson obviously thinks highly of the Borlase volume: "This is
one of the most pleasing and elegant pieces of local enquiry that our
country has produced" (*LM*, I, 91). He is content, therefore, to produce
a thorough summary with almost no editorial comment. But the review
contains many examples of delightfully terse Johnsonian condensations:
for instance, Borlase comments that "In all such little Islands Spirituous
Liquors are too much used; but those that live temperate here, live to
a great age" (p. 67); Johnson merely says, "The inhabitants, if sober,
live long" (*LM*, I, 94).

The reviews of Warton and Jenyns differ from the review of Borlase
primarily in containing much editorial comment, but otherwise the
techniques are similar. For example, in discussing the pastoral poetry
of Pope, Warton says:

> Upon the whole, the principal merit of the PASTORALS of
> Pope consists, in their correct and musical versification;
> musical, to a degree of which rhyme could hardly be thought
> capable: and in giving the first specimen of that harmony in
> English verse, which is now become indispensably necessary;
> and which has so forcibly and universally influenced the
> publick ear, as to have rendered every moderate rhymer
> melodious [p. 10].

In condensing this passage, Johnson says that the chief beauty of the
Pastorals "consists in their *correct and musical versification, which
has so influenced the* English *ear, as to render every moderate
rhymer harmonious*" [*LM*, I, 35].

In another passage Warton says that "although the Alexandrine
may be supposed to be a modern measure, yet I would remark, that
it was first used or invented by Robert of Glocester, whose poem
consists entirely of Alexandrine verses, with the addition of two
syllables" [p. 150]. Johnson condenses this by saying that "*the
alexandrine may be thought a modern measure, but that* Robert
of Gloucester's *verse is an alexandrine, with the addition of two
syllables*" [*LM*, I, 37].

This review of less than four pages is concise yet detailed and thorough. Its subject engages Johnson's attention and interest, and he brings to it a wealth of information and mature opinion. In the last paragraph of the review, Johnson says that "in this extract it was thought convenient to dwell chiefly upon such observations as relate immediately to *Pope*, without deviating with the author into incidental inquiries" [*LM*, I, 38]. He does this admirably and displays great skill in selecting interesting and pertinent passages from the mass of Warton's digressions. On another page Johnson states that Warton "proceeds on examining passage after passage of [the *Essay on Criticism*]; but we must pass over all these criticisms to which we have not something to add or to object, or where this author does not differ from the general voice of mankind" [*LM*, I, 37]. By choosing many passages to which he can object, Johnson creates the aura of contention which adds so much to the quality of his best reviews. Also, the subject matter of the book lends itself to the type of generalized comments which Johnson makes so well — see, for example, the passage which begins, "I cannot forbear to hint to this writer and all others the danger and weakness of trusting too readily to information" [*LM*, I, 37], or the passage which ends, "Young men in haste to be renowned too frequently talk of books which they have scarcely seen" [*LM*, I, 37]. All of these elements combine to produce a review which is interesting, well written and informative.

While admiring these merits of the review, one is intrigued to note that Johnson neglects completely the main point of Warton's book, which is a thorough, "pre-Romantic" attack on Pope's poetry. In the dedication to Edward Young, Warton says that "The Sublime and the Pathetic are the two chief nerves of all genuine poesy. What is there very sublime or very Pathetic in POPE?" (p. x). He then discusses four classes of poets, and closes by saying "In which of these classes POPE deserves to be placed, the following work is intended to determine" (p. xii). Obviously, Warton finds very little of the sublime or pathetic in Pope's poetry, and he closes his volume by remarking that "the reputation of POPE, as a poet, among posterity, will be principally owing to his WINDSOR-FOREST, his RAPE OF THE LOCK, and his ELOISA TO ABELARD; whilst the facts and characters alluded to and exposed, in his later writings, will be forgotten and unknown, and their poignancy and propriety little relished. For WIT and SATIRE are transitory and perishable, but NATURE and PASSION are eternal" (p. 334).

One may only suppose that since Johnson disagreed so strongly both with this definition of poetry and with the estimate of Pope's poetry, and since Johnson was a friend of Warton's, that he decided

merely to discuss other aspects of the book in his review in the
Literary Magazine. However, in 1781 when Johnson was writing his
"Life of Pope," he undoubtedly knew that Warton was then preparing
the second volume of his *Essay on . . . Pope.* It has always seemed to
me that Johnson had Warton specifically in mind in the great perora-
tion of his "Life of Pope":

> After all this, it is surely superfluous to answer the question
> that has once been asked, Whether Pope was a poet? otherwise
> than by asking in return, If Pope be not a poet, where is poetry
> to be found? To circumscribe poetry by a definition will only
> shew the narrowness of the definer, though a definition
> which shall exclude Pope will not easily be made. Let us
> look round upon the present time, and back upon the past;
> let us enquire to whom the voice of mankind has decreed
> the wreath of poetry; let their productions be examined,
> and their claims stated, and the pretensions of Pope will
> be no more disputed.[13]

This, surely, is the type of response one had hoped to find in the
review of 1756.

The review of Jenyns' *Free Inquiry* contains a few examples of
"quotations" typical of Johnson. For instance, the second paragraph
of the review begins with this sentence:

> In the first letter *on evil in general,* he observes, that 'it is
> the solution of this important question, *whence came evil,*
> alone, that can ascertain the moral characteristic of God,
> without which there is an end of all distinction between
> good and evil' [*LM*, II, 171].

The sentence within quotation marks seems fairly simple and direct,
yet Johnson composed it by conflating three phrases: Jenyns, page
3, lines 17–19; page 3, line 1; and page 5, lines 10–11. Johnson
rearranged his material, added two words —"without which" —
and created the quotation.

In another passage Jenyns mentions the "supposition of a Being
originally perfect, and yet capable of rendering itself wicked and
miserable, is undoubtedly a Contradiction, that very power being
the highest Imperfection imaginable" [p. 99]. Johnson merely says
that man's *"rendering himself wicked and miserable is the highest
imperfection imaginable"* [*LM*, II, *303* — misnumbered 305].

At the conclusion of Letter V, Jenyns says:

> . . . what has here been said of their imperfections,
> and abuses, is by no means intended as a defence of them,

but meant only to shew their necessity: to this every
wise man ought quietly to submit, endeavouring at the
same time to redress them to the utmost of his power . . .
[p. 149].

In Johnson's review, this passage, placed within quotation marks,
reads: "What has here been said of their imperfections and abuses, is
by no means intended as a defence of them: every wise man ought to
redress them to the utmost of his power" [*LM*, II, *304* — misnumbered
306].

These examples of adapting and condensing are not typical of this
review, however; this is Johnson's longest review, and he made it so
by quoting a great many passages, extensively and verbatim. The
review reproduces so many typographical features of the book — such
as unusual spellings — that it seems likely that Johnson simply marked
passages in the book and gave it to the printer for copy. In one instance
Johnson reproduces verbatim thirteen consecutive pages from the book
[Jenyns, pp. 83—95; *LM*, II, *300—302* — misnumbered 302—304]; in
another passage he quotes verbatim five consecutive pages [Jenyns,
pp. 54—58; *LM*, II, 253, *299* — misnumbered 301].

This is an excellent review for many reasons. The reader learns in
great detail of the contents of the book; Jenyns' ideas are presented,
analyzed, and evaluated.[14] In addition to Johnson's discussion of such
intellectual concepts as the great chain of being, the reader also is
presented with Johnson's comments on poverty, on educating the
poor, on human suffering, on subordination, and on the value of
writing. (From this review one learns a great deal about Samuel
Johnson as well as Soame Jenyns.) Once again, the subject matter
of the book leads Johnson into excellent, generalized discussions and
comments — see, for example, the passage which begins, "The bulk of
mankind is not likely to be very wise or very good" [*LM*, II, 174]; or
the passage which begins, "I am always afraid of determining on the
side of envy or cruelty" [*LM*, II, 175]; or the passage which begins,
"*Poverty* is very gently paraphrased by *want of riches*" [*LM*, II,
174]; or his supremely effective analogy, which begins, "I cannot
resist the temptation of contemplating this analogy, which I think
he might have carried further very much to the advantage of his
argument. He might have shewn that these *hunters whose game is man*
have many sports analagous to our own" [*LM*, II, *300* — misnumbered
302]. Johnson's wisdom, common sense, broad experience, and
humane compassion are perhaps nowhere displayed to better advantage than in these discussions. In this review we also enjoy the high
quality of Johnson's prose; many passages are vivid and memorable —
for example: "[The poor] are not pained by casual incivility, or

mortified by the mutilation of a compliment; but this happiness is
like that of a malefactor who ceases to feel the cords that bind him
when the pincers are tearing his flesh" [*LM*, II, 174]. This review
also has the benefit of intense, dramatic controversy, and we rejoice
to see Johnson crush his opponent so completely.

   And yet, our feelings about this last point are surely ambivalent,
for Johnson triumphs in such a way that it tends to mar the review.
He engages in direct *ad hominem* attacks to a greater degree than in
any of his other writings, and these attacks lack the lightness of
touch and tone characteristic of his remarks on Hanway. For example,
in the fifth paragraph Johnson says:

> I am told, that this pamphlet is not the effort of hunger;
> What can it be then but the product of vanity? and yet how
> can vanity be gratified by plagiarism, or transcription? When
> this speculatist finds himself prompted to another performance,
> let him consider whether he is about to disburthen his mind
> or employ his fingers; and if I might venture to offer him
> a subject, I should wish that he would solve this question,
> Why he that has nothing to write, should desire to be
> a writer [*LM*, II, 171].

Johnson overburdens Jenyns with ironic and sarcastic remarks —
e.g., by mentioning "the diligent researches of this great investigator"
[*LM*, II, 172]. Even when Johnson discovers a statement which he
believes "is certainly just," he says that he will "insert it, not that
it will give any information to any reader, but it may serve to shew
how the most common notion may be swelled in sound, and diffused
in bulk, till it shall perhaps astonish the author himself" [*LM*, II
251].

   Just as Johnson was known on occasion to "talk for victory,"
apparently in this instance he yielded to the urge to "review for
victory." As a result he became overly zealous, and this in turn caused
him to be repetitious. He could not make a point and leave it but had
to come back to it whenever Jenyns did. For example, Johnson discusses the great chain of being quite adequately on pages 171–73,
and yet thousands of words later he says:

> I have already spent some considerations on the *scale of
> being*, of which yet I am obliged to renew the mention when-
> ever a new argument is made to rest upon it, and I must
> therefore again remark . . . [*LM*, II, *303* — misnumbered
> 305].

Johnson is even more repetitious in insisting that the problem of the origin of evil is beyond human understanding, and thus any human who dares to discuss the subject is foolish and presumptuous. In pursuing these points, Johnson lets the review become too long and somewhat disorganized. It is no excuse to argue that the review is merely reflecting the repetition and lack of structure in Jenyns' book.

What might cause Johnson to become so zealous in this review? I assume that intellectual disagreement over such matters as the great chain of being would not be sufficient cause; he disagrees with Pope on the same subject, and yet in none of his writings does he subject Pope to this sort of treatment. Nor can the fact that Jenyns is a poor writer be sufficient cause; Johnson reviewed many worse writers (including Hanway), but he treats none of them with such severity.

One possible reason might be Jenyns' character. Edmond Malone records this account:

> Mr. Soame Jenyns, who died a few days ago, had (as Mr. Wm. Gerard Hamilton, who sat for six years at the Board of Trade with him, informed me) no notion of ratiocination, no rectitude of mind; nor could he be made without much labour to comprehend an argument. If however there was anything weak, or defective, or ridiculous in what another said, he always laid hold of it and played upon it with success. He looked at everything with a view to pleasantry alone. This being his grand object, and he being no reasoner, his best friends were at a loss to know whether his book upon Christianity was serious or ironical.[15]

Undoubtedly Johnson was morally offended by the book and its author. That Jenyns was a trifler is apparent from the book, whether or not Johnson had any personal knowledge of his character. Surely Johnson hoped that if he were severe enough in his review he might counteract the influence of the book and might prevent Jenyns from dabbling again.

* * * * *

In his review of Jenyns' *Free Inquiry*, Johnson comments:

> Many of the books which now croud the world, may be justly suspected to be written for the sake of some invisible order of beings, for surely they are of no use to any of the corporeal inhabitants of the world. Of the productions of the last bounteous year, how many can be said to serve any purpose of use or pleasure [*LM*, II, *300* — misnumbered 302].

94

One cannot blame Johnson for looking with a jaundiced eye at the books published during the period in which he reviewed books for the *Literary Magazine*. Comparatively few — including some that he chose to review — could meet his criteria of usefulness or pleasure. But the same cannot be said of the reviews he wrote for the magazine during this time, for a majority of them still seem fresh, well-written, and interesting, displaying Johnson's characteristic vigor and "nervousness." They constitute, collectively, a piece of writing which has more breadth and variety than anything else which ever came from Johnson's pen (with the obvious exception of the *Dictionary*). They are, so far as I know, the only group of early book reviews which are still read for literary pleasure in addition to historical and literary researches.

Johnson seems to have been an ideal book reviewer. He read omnivorously and had a remarkable memory which enabled him to recall with accuracy passages from books he had not seen in years. His keen critical faculties were usually employed in a fair, even-handed manner; they were not blunted by an unthinking adherence to a cause or sect. Since he lived in an age before the onset of specialization, he wrote with ease and enthusiasm about chemistry or travel books, natural history or politics, tea drinking or poetry. His strength of mind and his broadly humane approach to life and literature are nowhere better displayed than in his reviews.

Approximately two-thirds of the book reviews currently accepted as Johnson's may be found in the pages of the *Literary Magazine*, and reading them is a richly rewarding experience. They are recommended to anyone who wishes to become better acquainted with the historical events of 1756–57, to observe the techniques of a fine reviewer, to share with him the wide variety of a year's reading, to learn more of Johnson's personal and critical opinions, or merely to enjoy much good writing.

NOTES TO CHAPTER I

[1] Recto of advertisement leaf attached to the first issue. Italics are not indicated.

[2] See, for example, the list in *CBEL*, II, 677–78.

[3] *Johnsonian Miscellanies*, ed. G. B. Hill (Oxford: Clarendon Press, 1897), I, 413–14. Also see the *Letters of Samuel Johnson*, ed. R. W. Chapman (Oxford: Clarendon Press, 1952), nos. 98.1 and 115.1 (Addenda, p. 426).

[4] *The Life of Samuel Johnson, LL.D.* (1st ed.; London, 1787), p. 351.

[5] See Appendix A, below. Also, Arthur Murphy in his review of Hawkins' *Life of Johnson* (*Monthly Review*, 76 [May, 1787], 372) confirms the statement that Faden was the printer of the magazine.

[6] See Appendix A, below.

[7] John Nichols says of Griffith Jones: "In the Literary Magazine with Johnson, and in the British Magazine with Smollett and Goldsmith, his anonymous labours were also associated . . . but as he rarely, if ever, put his name to the productions of his pen, they cannot now be traced" (*Literary Anecdotes of the Eighteenth Century* [1812], III, 465). Allen T. Hazen correctly states (p. 127) that "Gordon Goodwin, in his biography of Jones in the *Dictionary of National Biography*, seems to have elaborated this remark into a suggestion that Jones was the printer of the *Literary Magazine*." There is apparently no reason for accepting Goodwin's suggestion.

[8] *Letters*, ed. Chapman, nos. 98.1 and 115.1 (Addenda, p. 426).

[9] *Monthly Review*, 77 (July, 1787), 70. Murphy's review of Hawkins' *Life* appeared in four installments: 76 (April and May, 1787), 273–92, 369–84; 77 (July and August, 1787), 56–70, 131–40. For confirmation of Murphy's authorship, see Benjamin Christie Nangle, *The Monthly Review, First Series 1749–1789. Indexes of Contributors and Articles* (Oxford: Clarendon Press, 1934), pp. 30, 134.

[10] *DNB*, 40 (1894), 313.

[1] *Ibid.* For further confirmation, see Arthur Murphy in the *Monthly Review*, 76 (May, 1787), 373; and the *Yale Edition of the Works of Samuel Johnson*, II (New Haven, 1963), xvii–xix.

[2] There were apparently nine original shares in the *London Chronicle*. For verification that Benjamin Collins was one of the original partners, see Charles Welsh, *A Bookseller of the Last Century* (London, 1885), p. 336 — hereafter cited as Welsh. The same source states that Newbery owned a one-ninth share at the time of his death. It seems likely that it was an original share. In fact, in the normal course of their business transactions, Newbery probably handled business matters in London both for himself and his Salisbury partner, Collins.

For evidence that Robert Dodsley was an original partner, see Ralph Straus, *Robert Dodsley* (London, 1910), p. 96 — hereafter cited as Straus. Dodsley formally withdrew as a partner on Jan. 24, 1757. For his letter of withdrawal, see Straus, pp. 98–99.

William Strahan was the printer of the *London Chronicle*. According to J. A. Cochrane, "Strahan may have been one of the partners from the paper's inception or he may have bought Dodsley's holding; he certainly owned a one-ninth share at the time of his death" (*Dr. Johnson's Printer: The Life of William Strahan* [Cambridge, Mass., 1964], p. 104). Strahan, however, apparently was not an original partner. According to his own ledgers (ledger "J," as marked by Professor William B. Todd), Strahan bought his one-ninth of the *London Chronicle* "from the Partnership" for £20 on Nov. 12, 1757.

J. Richardson and William Innys probably were original partners in the newspaper. William Strahan apparently acted as treasurer for the group of owners, for his ledgers frequently record the payment of quarterly dividends to Newbery, Collins, Richardson, and Innys. The earliest record I found for paying Innys and Richardson was an entry dated June, 1759 recording the payment of August, 1758 (British Library Add. MSS. 48800, folio 89), but the two may have been partners in 1757 as well. The absence of earlier entries is not necessarily significant. There must have been some other method of payment prior to Nov., 1757 when Strahan bought into the partnership.

Another person who may have owned an original share was Mr. Spens, the editor of the newspaper at its inception, whose editorial policies soon aroused Dodsley's wrath (Straus, pp. 96–99). This is probably the same Mr. C. Spens who, in 1754, entered into "a treaty of partnership" with William Bowyer and his relative James Emonson (Nichols, *Literary Anecdotes*, II [1812], 260). Nichols also states that when this partnership broke up in July, 1757, Emonson opened a printing office in St. John's Square and began printing a new evening paper

entitled *Lloyd's Evening Post and British Chronicle*, the editor of which
was C. Spens.

Perhaps Spens, as his relationship with Bowyer began to go sour
(Nichols, p. 260), agreed to edit the *London Chronicle* beginning Jan.
1, 1757. However, eleven issues under Spens's editorship were enough
to infuriate Dodsley to the point of withdrawing from the partnership.
It is possible that in the following months some of the other partners
may have become equally disturbed about Spens. Therefore, in July
when Spens became editor of *Lloyd's Evening Post*, he may well have
left his controversial position with the *London Chronicle*. If so, it is
probable that this is the time at which Griffith Jones began his long
and successful editorship of the *London Chronicle* (see note 14 below).

In summary, my suggestion is that the nine original partners in
the *London Chronicle* were John Newbery, Benjamin Collins,
J. Richardson, William Innys, Robert Dodsley, C. Spens, John Wilkie,
Griffith Jones, and William Faden.

¹³ See footnote 5 above; Plomer, *Dictionary*, pp. 87–88; and the
imprints of the periodicals.

¹⁴ John Wilkie's name appears on the imprint of the *London
Chronicle* from Jan. 1, 1757 through Mar. 20, 1781, when it is
replaced by T. Wilkie [his son?]. Wilkie died on July 2, 1785
(Plomer, p. 264). Griffith Jones is frequently referred to as the editor
of the *London Chronicle* (for example, see Nichols, *Literary Anecdotes*,
III [1812], 465 and the index of the *Private Papers of James Boswell
from Malahide Castle* . . . 18 vols.; Privately printed for Ralph Isham,
1928–34). In his *Papers*, Boswell often refers to both Jones and
Wilkie: e.g., Saturday May 2, 1772: "Dined Mitre with Jones and
Wilkie" [X (1930), 261]; Monday May 6, 1776: "Wilkie and Jones
disappointed you" [XI (1931), 270]; Tues., March 16, 1779: ". . . I
went first and sat a little with Mr. Jones, who told me he had been
ill and had now given up being the Conductor of 'The London
Chronicle' " [XIII (1932), 210]. According to the *DNB*, Jones died
on Sept. 12, 1786.

¹⁵ Nichols, *Literary Anecdotes*, III (1812), 465.

¹⁶ Welsh, *A Bookseller of the Last Century*, pp. 39, 336.

¹⁷ Numbers 1–5 were published every Sat. – Sept. 17 through
Oct. 15, 1757; numbers 6–30 were published every Thurs. – Oct. 20,
1757 through April 6, 1758. These essays were then revised and
reprinted in two volumes, 12°, with this imprint: *LONDON:* / Printed
for J. WILKIE, behind the *Chapter-House*, in / *St. Paul's Church-Yard.*
M.DCC.LVIII. / [Price Six Shillings.] These two volumes were published on April 27, 1758 (*Public Advertiser; Whitehall Evening Post*,
April 25–27). The pseudonymous author was Stentor Telltruth,
whose real identity remains unknown.

[18] See the *Collected Works of Oliver Goldsmith*, ed. Arthur Friedman (Oxford: Clarendon Press, 1966), I, 345.

[19] Plomer, *Dictionary*, p. 264.

[20] Dodsley, it may be noted, was not totally averse to periodicals — e.g., he had hired Mark Akenside to edit *The Museum* for him. There is no doubt, however, that his main interest lay in books — specifically, in the mid 1750's, with such a major item as his own famous *Collection of Poems*. Strahan's ledgers show that he, Collins, and Newbery were partners in *Lloyd's Evening Post*. Strahan also was a partner in the *Monthly Review*, but apparently not with any members of the group being discussed here.

[21] Certainly some of these men, especially Newbery, were also very active in publishing books; but during this period their involvement in periodicals seems remarkable.

[22] See Chapter II, below, item no. 4.

[23] See my Preface above.

[24] *Letters*, ed. Chapman, nos. 32, 33, 34.

[25] See the *Daily Advertiser* of that date.

[26] See above, note 11.

[27] *The Yale Edition of the Works of Samuel Johnson*, II (New Haven, 1963), xviii. For detailed evidence of Newbery's probable interest in the newspaper, see Gwin J. Kolb, "John Newbery, Projector of the *Universal Chronicle*: A Study of the Advertisements," *SB*, 11 (1958), 249–51.

[28] *Life*, I, 350, n. 3.

[29] Gwin J. Kolb, "Dr. Johnson and the *Public Ledger*: A Small Addition to the Canon," *SB*, 11 (1958), 252–55.

[30] *Ibid.*, p. 253 and n. 4.

[31] Hazen (p. 251) gives a Chronological List of works for which Johnson wrote prefaces or dedications. Not including three items which Hazen rejects, the list includes twenty works published between 1756 and 1763. Thirteen of these were published by J. Payne, J. Newbery, J. Richardson, W. Faden, or J. Wilkie (although some of the imprints include additional names).

[32] John Newbery was known as a shrewd advertising man, and I suspect that in some books he used the list of subscribers for advertising purposes. In addition to the list of genuine but undistinguished subscribers, Newbery might gratuitously add the names of friends and members of his "syndicate," names of prestige and weight in the world of books. For instance, in William Woty's *The Shrubs of Parnassus* (1760), the list of subscribers includes: Mr. Bowyer; Mr. Collins of Salisbury; Mr. Emonson; Mr. Faden; Mr. Griffith Jones; Arthur Murphy; "Mr. Newbery, St. Paul's Church Yard, 6 Books";

Mr. J. Payne; Dr. Smollett; Mr. Charles Spens; Mr. Strahan; and "Samuel Johnson, A.M.," standing at the head of the list under "J."

One must not be cynical about this, especially where proof is lacking. Probably most subscription lists are completely genuine, as are most of the names on any subscription list. But, when a list of subscribers is included in the trade edition of a completely undistinguished book, and when that list includes the well-known names of the publisher's business associates, then I wonder if all of them actually paid the subscription price.

See my discussion of this point in *Eighteenth-Century English Books* (Chicago: Association of College and Research Libraries, 1976), pp. 34–41, and the rejoinder of Herman W. Liebert in the same volume.

[33] Newspaper advertisements for the first issue of the magazine in May, 1756 say that it is "Printed for the Proprietors, sold by W. Faden." See Appendix A below.

[34] See note 12 above.

[35] *Johnsonian Miscellanies*, I, 413.

[36] 1st ed.; London, 1787, p. 351.

[37] *Life*, I, 307. Greene (p. 367) is undoubtedly correct in assuming that Boswell's statement derives from a passage in the *European Magazine*, 7 (Feb., 1785), 83, which states: "The intire superintendence of the performance, during 15 numbers, fell to the share of Dr. Johnson . . . ."

[38] See, for example, Courtney's *Bibliography*, pp. 75–77; *CBEL*, II, 619–20; Greene's article; and Bloom, pp. 89–112, 267–69.

[39] *Letters*, ed. Chapman, no. 98.1.

[40] *Public Advertiser*, 5 Jan. 1756 (as quoted by Hazen, p. 128).

[41] *Daily Advertiser*, 15 May 1756. See Appendix A, below.

[42] *Letters*, ed. Chapman, nos. 77, 78, 90, 96.

[43] Ralph Straus, *Robert Dodsley* (London, 1910), pp. 82–83.

[44] Letter from Stuart Piggott, *TLS*, June 13, 1929. Also, see my introduction to the *Universal Visiter*, reproduced as a volume in this series.

[45] I quote Arthur Friedman, *Collected Works of Oliver Goldsmith*, II (1966), ix.

[46] W. J. Bate in the *Yale Edition of the Works of Samuel Johnson*, II, (1963), xix. In his *Life*, Hawkins states that Johnson had "a share in the profits of this paper" (1st ed.; London, 1787, p. 363).

[47] *Letters*, ed. Chapman, no. 113. Johnson's life of Sir Thomas Browne, prefixed to the second edition of *Christian Morals*, was published March 18, 1756. See Chapter II, below, item no. 14.

[48] *Johnsonian Miscellanies*, I, 398.

[49] See Chapter II, below, item no. 38.

[50] For a more detailed presentation of these points, see Greene's *The Politics of Samuel Johnson* (New Haven, 1960), especially pp. 154–72.

[51] I quote Duncan E. Isles, "Unpublished Johnson Letters," *TLS*, July 29, 1965, p. 666.

[52] See Chapter II, below, item no. 22.

[53] Preface to Vol. XVI (1746). It may be noted that in 1756 even such a successful publication as the *Monthly Review* had a monthly circulation of 2,500 copies. In fact, its circulation did not increase to 2,750 copies until the issue of July, 1766 (British Library Add. MSS. 48800, folios 95, 111, 114, 118, 119, 132 and 140).

[54] These ways are listed in Appendix A, below.

[55] See Appendix A, below.

[56] See Chapter II, below, item no. 37.

[57] The description of Johnson as "a truly good Man, and very able Writer" suggests that this brief article may have been inserted in the *London Chronicle* by Arthur Murphy, who was writing for both the newspaper and the magazine at this time. Since both were published the same day, the newspaper necessarily had prior knowledge of the review. (This issue of the magazine, for example, contains Murphy's review of Burke's *Sublime and Beautiful*.) Such praise is typical of Murphy: see, for example, the "splendid encomium" of Johnson with which he introduces Johnson's proposals for an edition of Shakespeare in the *London Chronicle*, April 12–14, 1757.

[58] *Review of English Studies*, N.S., 27 (1976), 17–26.

[59] Unfortunately, no copy of the *Gazetteer* of this date seems to be in existence. See Chapter II, below, item no. 39; also, McClure, p. 19, n. 3.

[60] *Life*, I, 314.

[61] Although the third installment of Johnson's review of Soame Jenyns' *Free Inquiry* was published in the next issue of the magazine, I assume that Johnson probably wrote the entire review as a single piece and turned in all the copy to the magazine even before the first installment was printed.

[62] *Letters*, ed. Chapman, no. 113.

[63] The late John D. Gordan, Curator of the Berg Collection in the New York Public Library, kindly allowed me to examine the library's extensive holdings of Burney manuscripts and notebooks. It was an exciting search, even though ultimately disappointing. The late James M. Osborn of New Haven informed me that there are no such materials in his Burney collection. Professor Joyce Hemlow of

McGill University assures me that she has never found any such items in her examination of all known Burney materials.

[64] See his article in *RES* (1956), especially pp. 367—73; also his more detailed and comprehensive discussion, "The Development of the Johnson Canon," *Restoration and Eighteenth-Century Literature: Essays in Honor of Alan Dugald McKillop* (Chicago: University of Chicago Press, 1963), pp. 407—27 — hereafter cited as "Greene, 'Development.' " I am indebted to him for his study of early attributions.

[65] *RES*, 7 (1956), 368, 372.

[66] I count as a review Johnson's reply to Hanway's paper in the *Gazetteer* of May 26, 1757, since, although it is not by itself a review, it forms an integral part of Johnson's criticism of Hanway's book.

[67] See his article in *RES*, 7 (1956), 385; and his "Development," p. 425.

[68] "A Possible Addition to the Johnson Canon," *RES*, New Series, 6 (Jan., 1955), 70—71.

[69] *RES*, 7 (1956), 389.

[70] 14 (May, 1756), 369—85.

[71] 1 (July, 1756), 489—508. For confirmation that Francklin wrote the review, see Derek Roper, "Smollett's 'Four Gentlemen': The First Contributors to the *Critical Review*," *RES*, 10 (Feb., 1959), 38—44.

[72] *Literary Magazine*, I, no. IX, 449.

[73] *Literary Magazine*, I, no. III, 132.

[74] In the *Gentleman's Magazine*, 30 (Oct., 1760), 453—56. This parallel was first noticed by Greene, p. 483.

[75] See Greene, p. 381.

[76] *London Chronicle*, Jan. 22—25, 1757, p. 85.

[77] Straus, *Robert Dodsley*, pp. 97—98.

[78] "The Newspaper," in *Johnson's England* (1933), II, 348.

[79] *Literary Magazine*, I, no. IX, 453.

[80] *Ibid.*, p. 461.

[81] *Literary Magazine*, II, no. X (1757), 31.

[82] See, for example, Greene, pp. 371—72, 375.

[83] He expresses such sentiments often in his *Lives of the English Poets*: see, for example, the "Life of Congreve," p. 34; the "Life of West," p. 378; the "Life of Akenside," p. 451; and the "Life of Gray," p. 462. (All page numbers refer to the Oxford World's Classics edition, vol. II [1952].)

[84] Oxford World's Classics edition, II (1952), 30—31.

[85] *Life*, I, 402.

[86] *Literary Magazine*, II, no. XII (1757), 116.

[87] *Ibid.*, p. 120.

[88] Although the reviews of these five pamphlets are not distinctively titled, numbered, or signed, their unity of subject and their similar treatment by the reviewer make them form a cohesive "series." Thus, since Johnson reviewed the first four of the series, he probably reviewed the fifth also. See R. S. Crane's use of this argument in *New Essays by Oliver Goldsmith* (Chicago, 1927), p. xxxiv.

[89] Greene attributes seven additional reviews to Johnson:

(1)   A Letter from Joseph Ames to John Booth of Bernard's-Inn (*LM*, I, 77—78). Greene says (p. 389) that the paragraph of comment on this letter "is tantamount to a review," so he includes this item among the reviews.

(2)   Peter Whalley (ed.), *The Works of Ben Jonson* (*LM*, I, 169—71).

(3)   John Free, *A Sermon preached at St. John's, in Southwark, on the 29th of May, 1756* (*LM*, I, 186).

(4)   Bourchier Cleeve, *A Scheme for preventing a further Increase of the National Debt . . .* (*LM*, I, 188—91).

(5)   *An Account of the Conferences held, and Treaties made, between major-general Sir William Johnson, and the chief sachems and warriors of the Mohawks* [etc.] (*LM*, I, 191—93).

(6)   R. Lovett, *The Subtil medium proved . . .* (*LM*, I, 231—34).

(7)   Dr. Hoadly and Mr. Wilson, *Observations on a series of Electrical Experiments* (*LM*, I, 234—39).

Of these seven, the only one that I believe Johnson may have written is the review of Bourchier Cleeve's tract on the national debt. However, all the extracts used in the review are verbatim quotations and do not show any Johnsonian abridgements.

NOTES TO CHAPTER III

[1] R. W. Chapman, "Authors and Booksellers," in *Johnson's England* (Oxford: Clarendon Press, 1933), II, 310–30, especially p. 319.

[2] Boswell reports the following conversation:

We talked of the Reviews, and Dr. Johnson spoke of them as he did at Thrale's. Sir Joshua said, what I have often thought, that he wondered to find so much good writing employed in them, when the authors were to remain unknown, and so could not have the motive of fame. JOHNSON. 'Nay, Sir, those who write in them, write well, in order to be paid well' [12 April 1776. *Life*, III, 44].

[3] For example, in March 1769, John Hawkesworth did not know that Owen Ruffhead was a fellow reviewer for the *Monthly Review*; see my article, "John Hawkesworth: Book Reviewer in the *Gentleman's Magazine*," *PQ*, 43 (April, 1964), 223–38, especially pp. 225–26.

[4] *Sale Catalogue of Dr. Johnson's Library, with an Essay by A. Edward Newton* (New York and London, 1925), items 393 and 548. Of course, one can never argue that Johnson did not possess a book on the basis of the sale catalogue of his library; it abounds in such vaguely catalogued items as no. 630 "A bundle of plays," no. 631 "A large bundle of curious pamphlets in quarto," no. 632 "A ditto in octavo," no. 635 "26 odd volumes," or no. 636 "A large quantity of pamphlets in a box."

[5] *Literary Magazine*, I, no. VI (1756), 282.

[6] Accustomed as we are today to the casual disregard of official publication dates by both publishers and booksellers, it is perhaps surprising to see the strict attention paid to dates of publication by the book trade in the mid-eighteenth century. One aspect of this is the extreme care taken by publishers to keep the public informed of the exact date of publication of a work. A high percentage of the

books published at this time was publicized with the full range of
advertisements in the newspapers: "In the Press and speedily will be
publish'd . . ."; "Next Month will be publish'd . . ."; "Saturday next
will be publish'd . . ."; "Tomorrow will be publish'd . . ."; "This
Day is publish'd . . . ." For a discussion and a particular example of
this, see my note, "The Publication Date of the First Edition of
'Rasselas,' " *N & Q*, New Series, 9, no. I (Jan., 1962), 21–22.

[7] For a discussion of the nature of Johnson's duties on the
Magazine, see Chapter I, above.

[8] See Hazen, pp. 247–48. Arthur Sherbo, in "The Uses and
Abuses of Internal Evidence," *Bulletin of the New York Public
Library*, 63, no. I (January, 1959), 5–22, especially pp. 17–20,
lists objections to Johnson's authorship of the Preface. Of course,
the fact that Sherbo's objections are demonstrably either false or
groundless does not prove that Johnson wrote the Preface; that has
yet to be established.

[9] See *Letters*, ed. Chapman, no. 69.

[10] Hazen, pp. 146–51, 198–200, 15–16.

[11] *Life*, IV, 214–15. In an earlier passage Johnson is quoted as
saying that "when a man writes from his own mind, he writes very
rapidly. The greatest part of a writer's time is spent in reading, in
order to write: a man will turn over half a library to make one book"
(*Life*, II, 344).

[12] Much of my enjoyment in reading the books and the reviews
has derived from "watching" Johnson make these extracts. The
process is fascinating, and often more skill and thought are displayed
in it than in the brief critical comments that accompany the extracts.

F. P. Walesby, in editing the 1825 edition of Johnson's *Works*,
occasionally omitted the extracts in reprinting the reviews. This
practice saves space, but it deprives us of Johnson's carefully prepared
condensations and extracts. I hope that all future editors will print
all parts of any reviews they include in their books.

It may be noted that Johnson did not suddenly develop this
technique of making extracts when he became a book reviewer in
the *Literary Magazine* in 1756. At that time he had just spent years
preparing the *Dictionary*, and many of the quotations that Johnson
uses as examples have undergone this process of condensation. (See,
for example, Katharine C. Balderston, "Dr. Johnson's Use of William
Law in the Dictionary," *PQ*, 39 [July, 1960], 379–88, especially
page 382, in which she quotes Johnson's remarks in the Preface to
the *Dictionary* and summarizes the earlier studies of Gordon Haight,
Theodore Stenberg, and Arthur Sherbo.) Such experience with the
Dictionary was very helpful to him as a book reviewer. To be sure,

Johnson also used this technique with great skill both before and after the *Dictionary* (see Greene, p. 375).

¹³ Johnson's "Preface to Pope," in *Prefaces, Biographical and Critical, to the Works of the English Poets*, VII (London: J. Nichols *et al*, 1781), 331.

¹⁴ For a discussion of the intellectual background of Jenyns' book and Johnson's review, see (for example) Arthur O. Lovejoy, *The Great Chain of Being: A Study of the History of an Idea* (Cambridge, Mass.: Harvard University Press, 1936), especially Lecture VI; Basil Willey, *The Eighteenth Century Background: Studies on the Idea of Nature in the Thought of the Period* (London: Chatto and Windus, 1940), especially Chapter III; or, for a brief account, Joseph Wood Krutch, *Samuel Johnson* (New York: Henry Holt, 1944), pp. 163–66.

¹⁵ James Prior, *Life of Edmond Malone* (London: Smith, Elder & Co., 1860), p. 375.

APPENDIX A

THE *LITERARY MAGAZINE*
AND THE *LONDON CHRONICLE*

In this appendix I discuss briefly the *Literary Magazine* and *London Chronicle* and present in detail the long list of poems and articles of all types that were printed, sometimes simultaneously, in both publications. While some of these items also appeared in other contemporary periodicals, such as the *Gentleman's Magazine*, no other two periodicals of 1757–58 that I examined have nearly so much in common as the *Literary Magazine* and *London Chronicle*. Reasons for these similarities, and the men responsible for them, are discussed in Chapter I.

Allen T. Hazen's *Samuel Johnson's Prefaces & Dedications* is the basis for later comments on the *Literary Magazine* made by such writers as Greene and Bloom. The present discussion assumes a know-ledge of Hazen's work (see pages 125–31) and will present only corrections or additions to it. Although this necessitates a random presentation of comments, it will save much time for the reader acquainted with Hazen's work.

Hazen starts his account of the magazine by saying that the first number was published on "19 May 1756 (*Public Advertiser*)" (p. 125), but this date happens to be incorrect. Advertisements in the *Daily Advertiser* concerning the first appearance of the *Literary Magazine* are as follows: Wednesday, May 12 and Thursday, May 13: "*Next Saturday will be publish'd . . .*"; Friday, May 14: "*Tomorrow will be publish'd . . .*"; and Saturday, May 15: "*This day is publish'd . . . .*"

There are only four imprints in all three volumes of the *Literary Magazine*, and this fact has caused some confusion. Hazen (pp. 127–28) merely gives the information contained in these imprints: the title-page of the first number says that it is "Printed for W. Faden"; the title-page of volume I says "Printed for J. Richardson"; and the title-pages of volumes II and III say "Printed for J. Wilkie." Bloom (pp. 89–90 and 282, n. 2), however, draws certain conclusions from

these facts: he states that William Faden and J. Richardson united
to start the magazine; that if Faden "had any proprietary interest
beyond publishing the first number it has been concealed effectively";
and that "Faden apparently initiated the magazine, the first number
bearing his imprint as publisher, i.e., 'Printed for W. Faden.' The
remainder of Vol. I, however, was printed for Richardson. See *Prefaces*,
pp. 126–128." He concludes by stating that the first volume was
printed for Richardson and the second and third for John Wilkie.

The advertisements in the *Daily Advertiser* and other newspapers
greatly supplement Hazen's account, correct Bloom, and clarify the
whole matter of publishers. The advertisements of the first number
in May, 1756 say "Printed for the Proprietors, sold by W. Faden."
The first number itself, of course, has the imprint "Printed for
W. Faden." All the remaining numbers of volume I (numbers II–IX)
were merely advertised as "Printed for W. Faden." It was at this
point, in the middle of January, 1757, that J. Richardson took over.
Since he was the new publisher, when the index and title-page of
volume I were printed, they were "Printed for J. Richardson," as —
according to the newspaper advertisements — were the first ten
numbers of volume II (numbers X–XIX).[1] Number XX, the last
number of volume II, was advertised as "Printed for J. Wilkie"; and
since Wilkie was the new publisher, when the title-page of volume II
was printed, it bore his imprint. The last seven numbers of the magazine (i.e., all of volume III) were also advertised as "Printed for
J. Wilkie." Thus, of the twenty-seven monthly numbers, the first
nine were published by Faden, the next ten by Richardson, and only
the last eight by Wilkie — a publishing situation quite different from
what one infers by looking only at title-pages.

Hazen says that "the magazine appeared on or about the fifteenth
of each month (and) the last number appeared in July 1758 . . . .
The heading of each number, usually 'The Literary Magazine,' is in
January 1758 'The Literary and Antigallican Magazine' " (p. 128).[2]
In fact, the first twenty issues, which were numbered, did appear
about the middle of each month, but the last seven issues (volume III)
were not numbered and each of them appeared on the first day of
the following month — i.e., from February 1 through August 1, 1758.[3]
These innovations in the magazine were probably brought about by
J. Wilkie, the new publisher. Wilkie was also publisher of the *London
Chronicle* at this time, and the January 21–24, 1758 issue of the
newspaper contained an advertisement explaining his changes and new
plans for the *Literary Magazine* (see Plate III). In spite of his reasons
for adding "Antigallican" to the title, for some reason it was dropped
after one number.[4] His other plans, however, were executed fairly

ADVERTISEMENT

Concerning the New Plan of the LITERARY *and* ANTIGALLICAN MAGAZINE, *which at the Request of the Generality of its Readers* will, for the future, be published *at the Beginning, instead of the Middle, of every Month ; to begin with the First Number of the next Volume, which will be published the* First *of* February, 1758, *and continued regularly in that Manner throughout the Year.*

By J. W I L K I E, behind the Chapter-House, in St. Paul's Church-yard.

To the P U B L I C.

SINCE the Commencement of this Work the Practice of Magazining has been so greatly improved by certain Publications, that the Authors of this, think proper to make some Additions to their original Plan, but without any Variation from it, but such, as they hope, will make it more worthy of what always has been their principal Aim, the Approbation of the Public.

They apprehend that the Plan which they have laid down for the following Year, is more extensive than that of any Periodical Pamphlet of the same Nature ; and in order to save any farther Preamble, they think proper to lay before the Public the Manner in which they propose to conduct it.

Politics are more generally read in *England* than, perhaps, any other Subject, and they shall be admitted into this Work, but in a very different Manner than they are in any other, as we disclaim the hackney'd Practice of re-ecchoing Factions, and re-publishing Dullness.

Some of us have lived long enough to remember a Time when political Writing had both its *Dignity* and *Use.* The former was derived from its *Authors,* the latter from its *Object.* The Pen is the only decent, the only dutiful, and perhaps the only successful Weapon that Men of great Property as well as Parts can draw against an Object formidable to the Interests or Liberties of their Country. But no such Object now exists, nor has, for some Years past. The Spirit of Party in *Great Britain,* after many Ebullitions is now subsided, and our internal political Balance seems now to have recovered that equitable Poize which the Nature of our Constitution both prescribes and exemplifies. In the mean while we must be of Opinion that political Writing, even upon our domestic Affairs, is now, perhaps, more necessary than ever ; because the Public is now in a Temper more susceptible of Information than it was when prejudiced by national Distinctions, adopted by the Ignorant and fomented by the Designing of all Parties : But we apprehend that our present political Differences are not such as can justify Asperity of Treatment upon either Side.

We shall not, therefore, load our Pages with faithful Transcripts from all the Scurrility of Party-Writers, for our Intention is to relieve our Readers by generally giving an Abridgement of what they exhibit at large, with a proper Commentary of our own ; unless either the Importance of the Matter, or the

Elegance of the Composition shall render it a Kind of Sacrilege either to curtail or censure it. At the same time, and under the same Division of our Undertaking, we shall, every Month, present the Public with an Original Essay of our own, upon such political Subjects as are most immediately and really interesting.

The Spirit of political Writing at present ought to be that of the *Greek* rather than the *Roman* Philippics ; it ought to summon our Fellow-Subjects to the *Campus Martius* and not to the *Aventine* Mount. Our present Situation calls for the Attention of a Patriot rather than the Interposition of a Tribune ; it demands Unanimity more than Jealousy ; and the executive, rather than the declamatory Powers.

Philological Subjects shall compose the next Division of our Undertaking ; and it shall exhibit every Month, an Original Essay either of a Literary or Critical Nature, together with a succinct Account of all new Performances in the Republic of Letters.

We are next to account for the additional Title (that of ANTIGALLICAN) which we have given to this Undertaking. We cannot do this more effectually than by observing with great Concern, that the Interests of Literature seem to be as much endangered as those of *Great Britain,* from *French* Encroachments. They have led us to substitute *Reading* in the Place of *Study,* and to call it *Learning.* We have seen the Prostitutes of the Pen earn more by translating from the *French,* than they could, had the same Compositions been Originals. To the *French* it is owing that we have adopted *Fashion* for *Taste,* and that we mistake *Ornament* for *Beauty.* Classics are daily translating from the worst of their Translations by those who are incapable to construe a Sentence of the dead Languages, and sometimes in Compositions that are Original, the Decorations of the Engraver form all the Merit of the Author. *Coldness,* under the Pretext of Correctness, now covers every Defect of Genius, and the Name of the Patron is often held up against all Criticism upon the Performance of the Author.

To prevent, to expose, and, if possible, to reform those and a thousand other Epidemical Follies that bid fair to extinguish true Learning, is the present Design of our Undertaking. We have formerly had too great Experience of the public Candour to distrust it now. Secure of its Favour, the only Patronage we shall either court or cultivate, we shall despise the Attacks of envious Malice and impotent Dullness, but shall not wantonly provoke either. We shall readily and gratefully insert every Composition either of Prose or Verse that comes from Correspondents who can, in any Degree, merit the Approbation of the Public. A just Regard shall be shewn to every Discovery that may tend to promote Arts, Sciences, Manufactures, Commerce or Agriculture ; and *particular Attention will be paid* to the most rational of all our public Entertainments, those of the Theatre, in Pages appropriated to that Purpose.

Our last Division shall be dedicated to an Account of Public Occurrences, and to an Insertion of such Pieces both in Prose and Verse as cannot admit of being alter'd or abridg'd ; and here the Labour will be rather mechanical than intellectual, as its greatest Merit will consist in Exactness and Impartiality. To conclude, nothing shall be omitted in this Undertaking that can contribute to the Originality, Authenticity, and Variety of its Contents.

III. John Wilkie's new plan of the *Literary and Antigallican Magazine* in the *London Chronicle* of January 21—24, 1758

consistently through the publication of the last number on August 1, 1758.[5]

In addition to original contributions, there were several main sources of material for the magazine. In numbers III and V of volume I, twelve articles were reprinted from the *Philosophical Transactions* of the Royal Society, volume XLIX, Part I, for 1755.[6] One number in volume II (number XVI, 15 July to 15 August, 1757) reprinted four articles from the *Philosophical Transactions*, volume XLIX, Part II, for 1756.[7] In the last number (volume III [July, 1758], 310–12) there appeared an article from the *Philosophical Transactions*, volume L, Part I, for 1757. In three consecutive issues (numbers IX–XI, published January–March, 1757), the *Literary Magazine* printed two dozen articles which were translated and adapted from *l'Histoire et les Mémoires de l'Académie Royale des Sciences*. The vast majority of these articles, not one of which was printed with acknowledgment, were taken from the volume for the year 1752, although several were taken from volumes as early as 1741.[8] Finally, there is a third source of scientific material: six medical articles (*LM*, II, 283–89)[9] are all extracted and adapted, without acknowledgment, from *Medical Observations and Enquiries, By a Society of Physicians in London* (London, 1757). This was apparently a very popular and highly esteemed book, for extensive accounts of it also appeared in the *London Chronicle, Gentleman's Magazine, Monthly Review*, and *Critical Review*.

Starting in January, 1757, the principal source of material for the *Literary Magazine* was the *London Chronicle*[10] (and, not unexpectedly, the newspaper also reprinted quite a few pieces from the magazine). No discussion of the *London Chronicle* is needed here, for good accounts are readily available.[11] However, since a misprint in Hazen's account has been copied by a later writer (Bloom, p. 136), it should be noted that the *Chronicle* increased its price to two pence halfpenny in the issue of July 5–7, 1757 rather than 1759.[12]

The *Literary Magazine* offered nothing unique to the public except an unusual time of publication, and, as we have seen, it lost that advantage in January, 1758. Since it lasted only twenty-seven months, it presumably had a modest circulation. On the other hand, the *London Chronicle* had several new, attractive features (see D. Nichol Smith's account, mentioned above); and since it lasted for over sixty-five years, it probably had a strong, competitive position in its circulation. Both Johnson and Boswell thought highly of the *Chronicle*, and Boswell observed, when he was abroad, that it had "a more extensive circulation upon the Continent than any of the English newspapers" (*Life*, I, 318; II, 103). Since several people, both publishers and writers, were involved simultaneously with both periodicals (see

Chapter I), it was only natural that they should make use of the
newspaper to try to bolster the circulation of the magazine. They
tried to do this in several ways. First of all, they advertised the
magazine quite regularly in the *Chronicle* — usually, more frequently
than in other newspapers. In the second place, just as each number of
the magazine appeared, several of its more interesting pieces frequently
would be reprinted in the *Chronicle* and labelled "from the *Literary
Magazine.*" (As we will see in the list below, a number of items so
labelled appeared in the *Chronicle* even before a given number of
the magazine was published.)[13] In these reprints, the *Chronicle*
occasionally gave additional little "puffs" to the magazine. For
example, it once began a review and then said, in parentheses, that
it was quoting "a judicious and candid Writer in the Literary Magazine,
from whom we borrow this Article verbatim" (*LC*, February 19–22,
1757). Similarly, in another review, it prefaced a quotation from the
magazine by saying: "The masterly Writer who gives the Account of
Books, printed in the Literary Magazine, concludes his Extract . . .
by observing . . ." (*LC*, January 22–25, 1757). Another reprint was
introduced with these words: "The public is indebted for the following
ingenious Essay to the Literary Magazine" (*LC*, March 9–11, 1758).
Also, the newspaper once reprinted the words of a song, but added:
"See this Song set to Music in the *Literary Magazine* for this Month"
(*LC*, June 25–28, 1757). Such efforts seem obvious enough, and
I should add that I have never found an instance in which the *London
Chronicle* treats a reprint or extract from any other source in this
manner.

The third, and perhaps most obvious, way in which the editors of
the two periodicals tried to strengthen the magazine's circulation was
to reprint in the magazine interesting pieces from the *Chronicle*.
I believe the best way to show such similarities is merely to list them.

In the following list I omit everything contained in those sections
of the magazine presenting the normal news events of each day — the
Chronological Diary, the lists of marriages and deaths, and so on.
The contents of these sections are obviously taken from the newspapers,[14] and I see no reason for enumerating all such similarities.

This list is undoubtedly incomplete; but after comparing thousands
of pages of the *London Chronicle* and the *Literary Magazine* and
seeing how skillfully extracts can be used without any signs of
quotation or acknowledgment, I believe it would take infinite time
and patience to try to determine all the similarities. At any rate, the
list shows the main items that the two have in common. Each number
of the *Literary Magazine* is listed chronologically with its date of
publication, and under it is given the title (or description) of each

item which appeared either earlier or later in the *London Chronicle.*

Nothing in this list is to be considered a verbatim reprint unless it is so marked. All reviews are clearly labelled "Review of —— ——." Reviews that are dissimilar are so labelled. Similar reviews, which I believe may have been written by Johnson, are discussed in the text. Whenever I mention that "some different extracts" are used, I mean that the pieces are generally the same but that some material is either added or deleted according to the requirements of space in the periodical. I usually do not indicate discrepancies in extracts from periodical essays.

When the actual titles of pieces are used, they are placed in quotation marks. When for the sake of brevity a running-title is used, it is given in quotation marks within square brackets. My own descriptions of pieces are enclosed in square brackets. When the number of a page is italicized, it means either that the page lacks a number or that it is misnumbered.

NOTES

[1] Number XIV, however, was advertised as "Printed by W. Faden, for J. Richardson" (see *Daily Advertiser,* June 23, 1757), and this is the advertisement which led Hazen to state that the printer of the *Literary Magazine* "was probably Faden" (p. 128). I certainly agree. Richardson evidently did not approve of that wording, however, for the later advertisements — even for number XIV — merely say "Printed for J. Richardson."

[2] Hazen (p. 128) also mentions "the first number, for April 15 to May 15 . . ." and the Library of Congress card catalogue contains a similar error. In fact, the first number of the magazine merely says, "The Literary Magazine, For the Year 1756. Number I" (*LM,* I, 1), and no months or dates are mentioned. Furthermore, in this number the Historical Memoirs, Chronological Diary, List of Deaths, and List of Promotions (pp. 43—53) all contain information dating "From January 1, 1756," and only the list of the Price of Stocks (p. *54*) is dated "from the 15th of April to the 14th of May 1756."

[3] See the *London Chronicle* of March 30 — April 1, 1758 for the publication date of the March issue and the advertisements in the *Daily Advertiser* for the other six issues.

[4] Strangely enough, the *Daily Advertiser* continued to advertise it as the *Literary and Antigallican Magazine* through the publication

of the May number on June 1, 1758. Of course, Wilkie's newspaper, the *London Chronicle*, consistently advertised the magazine correctly.

⁵ In my opinion Wilkie made a mistake by changing the time of publication. By appearing in the middle of the month, the magazine often reviewed books that were published within the previous two weeks and it also printed articles on current news events. Since no other magazine was published at the same time of month, it had the advantage of being the first to appear with such recent items. But when the time of publication was changed to the first of the month, these features of the magazine were in simultaneous competition with the *Monthly Review, Critical Review, Gentleman's Magazine* and a horde of others. The net effect was probably an increase in competition which the *Literary Magazine* could ill afford.

⁶ Greene mentions these articles on pages 381 and 386. According to Boswell, this volume of the *Philosophical Transactions* was reviewed by Samuel Johnson (*LM*, I, number IV [15 July to 15 August, 1756], 193—97).

⁷ All four articles were printed without acknowledgment. See *LM*, II, 329—30, 333—37, 340—42, 352—55.

⁸ I have identified the specific sources for twenty-one of the articles; the sources for three have eluded me. (I assume that these three were also printed in the *Mémoires*, for they were written by contributing members of the Academy.) Frequently in the original French volumes, an author would write a series of two or three articles on related topics, and in the *Literary Magazine* these are usually abridged into one article. In the magazine, these twenty-four articles appear on the following pages: Volume I, 461—63, 463—64, 465—66, 466, 467, 467—68, 470—73, 473, 473—74, 474(2), 475; Volume II, 9—15, 15—17, 17—18, 18—19, 19—20, 21—22, 22—23, 26, 63—64, 64—65, 66—68, 73—75.

⁹ The article on pages 285—87 is a combination of two articles in the book, one by John Fordyce (*LM*, p. 285 to top of p. 287) and one by Dr. Fothergill (*LM*, p. 287), so counting these as two gives the total of six.

¹⁰ I do not include, of course, contemporary periodical essays, which are an obvious source of material and are always identified in the *Literary Magazine*. Occasionally a whole paper is reprinted, but more frequently extracts of varying length are given. The number of essays reprinted is as follows: from the *Monitor*, 11; *World*, 5; *Connoisseur, Test, Con-Test, Centinel*, and *Idler*, 3 each; *Herald*, 2; and *Humanist*, 1. (The *Herald; or, Patriot Proclaimer* was published in 30 weekly numbers from Sat., Sept. 17, 1757 through Thurs., April 6, 1758; it was printed for J. Wilkie. Also, while Bloom [p. 95]

mentions the reprinting of *Idler* numbers 6 and 15, it should be noted that number 1 was also reprinted [*LM*, III (April, 1758), 178–79].)

[11] See Hazen, pp. 131–32, and D. Nichol Smith's article in *Johnson's England* (Oxford, 1933), II, 345–49.

[12] For verification, see the *Chronicle* of that date; and for the increase in the stamp tax which caused the price change, see *Johnson's England*, II, 364.

[13] Even though the acknowledgments were worded in various ways, in my list I merely say, "from the *LM*." The only two items which the *Literary Magazine* acknowledges are reprinted from the *London Chronicle* I mark as "from the *LC*."

[14] Several volumes of newspapers, including the *London Chronicle*, in the University of Chicago Library have been marked in ink by editors who were using them for copy. The marked deletions and changes in capitalization, spelling, and sometimes wording present an interesting study in the editorial practices of 1757–58.

THE LITERARY MAGAZINE: OR, UNIVERSAL REVIEW (1756–58)

LM, I, number I. Published May 15, 1756 (*Daily Advertiser; London Evening-Post*)

LM, I, number II (May 15 to June 15, 1756). Published June 15, 1756 (*Public Advertiser*).

LM, I, number III (June 15 to July 15, 1756). Published July 15, 1756 (*Public Advertiser*).

LM, I, number IV (July 15 to August 15, 1756). Published August 16, 1756 (*Daily Advertiser; Public Advertiser*).

Review of Bourchier Cleeve's *Scheme for preventing a further increase of the National Debt*, pp. 188–91.

LC, March 5–8, 1757. Reprints review verbatim, "from the *LM*."

LM, I, number V (August 15 to September 15, 1756). Published September 15, 1756 (*Public Advertiser*).

LM, I, number VI (September 15 to October 15, 1756). Published October 15, 1756 (*Daily Advertiser*).

LM, I, number VII (October 15 to November 15, 1756). Published November 15, 1756 (*Public Advertiser*).

114 Appendix A

"Memoirs of the King of Prussia," pp. *327*–33.
LC, May 21–24, 1757. Reprinted verbatim, "from the *LM.*"

LM, I, number VIII (November 15 to December 15, 1756). Published December 16, 1756 (*General Evening Post*, Dec. 14–16, 1756).
[Memoirs of the King of Prussia], pp. *383*–90.
LC, May 24–26, 26–28, 1757. Reprinted verbatim, "from the *LM.*"

LM, I, number IX (December 15, 1756 to January 15, 1757). Published January 20, 1757 (*General Evening Post*, Jan. 18–20, 1757).
[Memoirs of the King of Prussia], pp. *439*–42.
LC, May 28–31, 1757. Reprinted verbatim, "from the *LM.*"

Review of Archibald Bower's *Answer to a scurrilous Pamphlet*, pp. 449–53.
LC, January 18–20, 20–22, 22–25, 1757. *LC* quotes last part of review, verbatim, "from the *LM.*" *LM* (pp. 449–50) gives same extract as *LC*, January 18–20.

The Test, no. 7, pp. 458–60
LC, January 1–4, 1757.

The Con-Test, no. 7, pp. 460–61.
LC, January 4–6, 1757.

["Anecdote of Richard Plantagenet"], pp. 464–65.
LC, January 20–22, 1757. Reprinted verbatim, "from the *LM.*"

[An Account of the Rantipole"], pp. 468–70.
LC, January 22–25, 1757. Reprinted verbatim, "from the *LM.*"

"An account of the trial of Admiral Byng," pp. 475–79.
LC, January 8–11, 11–13, 13–15, 1757. *LC* and *LM* occasionally use different extracts.

Colley Cibber's "Ode for the New Year," p. 482.
LC, January 1, 1757. Reprinted verbatim.

LM, II, number X (January 15 to February 15, 1757). Published February 17, 1757 (*Daily Advertiser* and *London Chronicle* and *General Evening Post*).

"An Account of Robert Francis Damien," pp. *1*–4.
LC, February 24–26, 1757. Quotes first paragraph only.

[Letters from Voltaire and Richelieu concerning Byng], pp. 7–8.
LC, February 1–3, 1757. Reprinted verbatim.

The Centinel, of January 27, 1757, pp. 20–21.
LC, February 1–3, 1757.

Review of William Whitehead's *Elegies with an Ode to the Tiber*, p. 31.
LC, February 19–22, 1757. Reprints review verbatim, "from the *LM*."

Review of David Hume's *Four Dissertations*, pp. 32–36.
LC, February 19–22, 22–24 and March 8–10, 1757. Also, see "The Theatre" in *LC*, February 22–24 and March 22–24, 1757.

Review of Tobias Smollett's *The Reprisal, or, The Tars of Old England*, pp. 36–38.
LC, January 29 – February 1, 1757. Prints the prologue. Also, the play is mentioned in "The Theatre," *LC*, February 1–3, 1757.

Review of Claude du Choisel's *Easy, short, and certain method of treating persons bit by mad animals*, pp. 38–39.
LC, January 1, 1757.

"Trial of Adm. Byng, continued from Vol. I," pp. 39–44.
LC, January 13–15, 18–20, 29 – February 1, 1757.
LC omits Byng's Defence.

"The Beer Drinking Briton," pp. 45–46.
LC, March 8–10, 1757. Reprinted verbatim, minus the music.

"Horace, Book III. Ode iii," p. 46.
LC, January 4–6, 1757. Reprinted verbatim.

LM, II, number XI (February 15 to March 15, 1757). Published March 16, 1757 (*Public Advertiser*). [Augustus Caesar to the married men of Rome], pp. 65–66.
LC, March 15–17, 1757.

"The Case of a distressed Family," p. 71.
LC, March 19–22, 1757. Reprinted verbatim, "from the *LM*."

Review of *The Connoisseur*, pp. 75–76.
LC, April 30 – May 3, 1757.

Review of Samuel Foote's *The Author*, pp. 76–79.
LC, February 15–17, 1757. Also, see "The Theatre," *LC* February 5–8, 8–10, 15–17, 1757.

["Resolutions of the Court Martial on Adm. Byng"], pp. 81–87.
LC, February 24–26, 1757. *LC* and *LM* occasionally use different extracts.

[Two pieces concerning *Douglas*: "Declamation from
the Presbytery of Edinburgh," and David Hume's
dedication of his *Four Dissertations*] , pp. 87–90.
LC, March 8–10, 1757. *LM* adds an introductory paragraph,
otherwise reprints *LC* verbatim.

"Extract from Dr. Birch's *History of the Royal Society*,"
p. 93.
LC, March 10–12, 1757. *LM* reprints extract verbatim.

"Ode to Friendship," pp. 94–95.
LC, March 15–17, 1757. Reprinted verbatim, "from the
LM."

LM, II, number XII (March 15 to April 15, 1757). Published April
16, 1757 (*Public Advertiser*). "A Description of the Grotto
of Antiparos," pp. 112–16.
LC, April 19–21, 1757. Reprinted verbatim, "from the *LM*."

Review of *An authentic and circumstantial Account of the
Confinement, Behaviour, and Death of Admiral Byng*,
pp. 116–20.
LC, April 2–5, 1757. *LC* and *LM* use some different
extracts.

Review of *Memoirs of the Marquis of Torcy*, pp. 120–26.
LC, May 3–5, 5–7, 7–10, 10–12, 1757.

Review of John Brown's *Estimate of the Manners and
Principles of the Times* (Vol. I), pp. 126–32.
LC, April 9–12, 14–16, 1757.

Review of John Dyer's *The Fleece*, pp. 134–36.
LC, March 22–24, 1757.

Review of John Home's *Douglas*, pp. 136–41.
LC, March 12–15, 22–24, 1757 (to mention the two
longest accounts).
See "The Theatre," *LC*, February 22–24, March 8–10,
10–12, 12–15, 15–17, 17–19, 19–22, 22–24, 1757.

"A Reflection," p. 143.
LC, April 21–23, 1757. Reprinted verbatim.

The Monitor, no. 90, April 9, 1757, pp. 145–47.
LC, April 14–16, 1757.

"Short, but serious Reasons for a National Militia," pp. 147–49.
Reprinted verbatim, "from the *LC*." *LC*, March 12–15, 1757.

"The Means of an Happy Life," pp. 151–52.
LC, April 21–23, 1757. Reprinted verbatim.

Prologue and Epilogue to *Douglas*, p. 152.
Reprinted verbatim.
LC, April 9—12, 1757.

Mr. Havard's "Ode to the Memory of Shakespeare," p. 153.
Reprinted verbatim.
LC, April 7—9, 1757.

"Elegy on the Death of Adm. Byng," p. 153.
Reprinted verbatim, "from the *LC*."
LC, April 2—5, 1757.

LM, II, number XIII (April 15 to May 15, 1757).
    Published May 17, 1757 (*Public Advertiser; London
    Chronicle*, May 14—17; *General Evening Post*, May 14—17).
    Review of Jonas Hanway's *Journal of Eight Days Journey* . . .,
    pp. 162—67.
    LC, June 4—7, 7—9, 11—14, 16—18, 18—21, 23—25, 25—28,
    1757.

    Review of Soame Jenyns' *Free Inquiry into the Nature and
    Origin of Evil*, pp. 171—75 [and continued on pp. 251—53,
    299—304 (misnumbered 301—306)].
    LC, April 12—14, 16—19, 1757. *LC* review very different
    from *LM*.

    "An Account of the Marine Society . . ." pp. 175—76.
    LC, May 7—10, 1757. Reprinted verbatim.

    ["Mr. Johnson's Proposal for an Edition of Shakespeare"] ,
    pp. 177—80.
    LC, April 12—14, 1757. The proposals are reprinted verbatim.

    Review of Lindsay's *The Evangelical History of Jesus Christ
    harmonized* . . . pp. 180—82.
    LC, May 17—19, 1757. The dedication is reprinted verbatim,
    and much else is very similar.

    Review of Edmund Burke's *Philosophical Enquiry into the
    Origin of our Ideas of the Sublime and Beautiful*, pp. 182—89.
    LC, June 9—11, 16—18, 21—23; July 7—9, 14—16, 1757.

    "Rational and easy methods to purify the Air, and regulate
    its heat in Melon-Frames and hot Green-houses," by Stephen
    Hales, pp. 191—92.
    LC, April 19—21, 1757. Reprinted verbatim.

    [Premiums offered by the Society for the Encouragement of
    Arts, Manufactures, and Commerce] , pp. 192—96.
    LC, April 23—26, 1757. Reprinted verbatim.

"Of the Art of laying out Gardens among the Chinese,"
pp. 199—201.
This extract from Chambers' book reprinted verbatim
from *LC*, April 28—30, 1757.

["A cheap Way to maintain a numerous Family"] ,
p. 202.
LC, April 30 — May 3, 1757. Reprinted verbatim.

LM, II, number XIV (May 15 to June 15, 1757). Published
June 17, 1757 (*Public Advertiser*).

["A Description of the City of Prague"] , pp. *217*—20
[and *273*—*75*] .
These extracts are from Edmund Chishull's *Description of
the City of Prague*, reviewed in *LC*, May 19—21, 1757 with
many of the same extracts.

Review of James Lind's *Essay on the most effectual means
of preserving the health of seamen in the royal Navy* . . .
pp. 225—28.
LC, August 11—13, 1757. Reprints review verbatim, "from
the *LM*."

Review of *Familiar Letters of Dr. William Sancroft* . . .
pp. 228—33.
LC, June 7—9, 1757. Many of the extracts are reprinted
verbatim.

Review of Daniel Peter Layard's *Essay on the nature, causes
and cure of the contagious distemper among the horned
cattle* . . . pp. 237—40.
LC, June 14—16, 16—18, 1757.

"An Account of the Loss of the Doddington Indiaman,"
pp. 250—51.
LC, June 4—7, 1757. Reprinted verbatim.

"The Hop Planter's Song," p. 258.
LC, June 25—28, 1757. Reprinted verbatim, minus the
music, "from the *LM*."

"Psalm CXLVIII. Paraphrased," p. 259.
LC, April 5—7, 1757. Reprinted verbatim.

"The Decision, A Tale," pp. 260—61.
LC, June 7—9, 1757. Reprinted verbatim.

LM, II, number XV (June 15 to July 15, 1757).
Published July 19, 1757 (*Public Advertiser*).

"Extract of the act for the better ordering of the militia forces in the several counties of that part of Great Britain called England," pp. 275–280. Reprinted verbatim from *LC*, June 30 – July 2, 1757.

["List of the Lord Lieutenants"] , p. 280.
LC, July 5–7, 1757. Reprinted verbatim.

Review of T. Gataker's *Observations on the internal Use of Solanum or Night-shade*, pp. 281–83.
Reprinted verbatim in *LC*, July 26–28, 1757, "from the *LM*."

[Six medical articles] , pp. 283–89.
Similar summaries and extracts are given in *LC*, May 26–28, 31 – June 2, and June 4–7, 1757.

Review of Robert Wood's *The Ruins of Balbec*, pp. 289–92 [and 342–45].
Similar extracts printed in *LC*, April 21–23, 1757.

The Monitor, June 3, 1757, pp. *296–98*.
LC, June 9–11, 1757. *LC* omits parts of first two paragraphs.

"An Essay on the private Life of the Romans . . ." pp. 305–07.
Reprinted verbatim in *LC*, July 16–19, 1757, "from the *LM*."

LM, II, number XVI (July 15 to August 15, 1757). Published August 16, 1757 (*London Chronicle*).
[An Essay on the private Life of the Romans] , pp. *321–29*.
Reprinted verbatim in *LC*, August 16–18, 18–20, 1757, "from the *LM*."

[Two letters from Camilla Paderni] , pp. 333–37.
LC, July 23–26, 26–28, 1757. Both *LC* and *LM* are quoting from the *Philosophical Transactions*, XLIX, Part II, for 1756 (1757), 490–504.

LM, II, number XVII (August 15 to September 15, 1757).
Published September 20, 1757 (*London Chronicle*).
[An Essay on the private Life of the Romans], pp. *361–67*.
Reprinted verbatim in *LC*, September 17–20, 20–22, 1757, "from the *LM*."

Review of *A full Answer to an infamous Libel* . . . pp. 381–86.
LC, September 8–10, 1757. Most of the extracts are identical in both.

Review of Theophilus Cibber's *The Auction*, pp. 393–94.
Reprinted verbatim in *LC*, September 20–22, 1757, "from the *LM*."

LM, II, number XVIII (September 15 to October 15, 1757).
Published October 18, 1757 (*Daily Advertiser* and *London Chronicle*).
Review of *A genuine account of the late grand Expedition to the coast of France* . . . pp. 414—19.
LC, October 8—11, 1757.

The Monitor, October 1, 1757, pp. 433—34. Similar summary and extracts printed in *LC*, October 6—8, 1757.

"To the good People of England," pp. 436—37.
LC, September 22—24, 1757. Reprinted verbatim.

"A Letter from a Gentleman at Bristol . . ." pp. 437—39.
LC, September 22—24, 1757. *LC* gives more extracts than *LM*.

["Petition of the E--- of C--- to his M---y"] , p. 440.
LC, September 27—29, 1757. Reprinted verbatim.

[Epitaph for King Theodore] , p. 442.
LC, October 1—4, 1757. Reprinted verbatim.

"A Song, Wrote extempore, by a young Lady," p. 442.
LC, October 8—11, 1757. Reprinted verbatim.

"Mr. Prior's Thought a little alter'd," p. 442.
LC, October 8—11, 1757. Reprinted verbatim.

LM, II, number XIX (October 15 to November 15, 1757).
Published November 19, 1757 (*London Chronicle*).
"P--b--gh's Ghost: Or a Veteran's Vision," pp. 457—62.
LC, November 15—17, 1757. Reprinted verbatim, "from the LM."

David Garrick's "To Mr. Gray, on his Odes," p. 468.
LC, September 29 — October 1, 1757. Reprinted verbatim.

"Letter from a Member of the Regency of Hanover . . ." pp. 480—85.
LC, November 17—19, 19—22, 1757. Reprinted verbatim, "from the *LM*."

The Monitor, November 12, 1757, pp. 485—87.
LC, November 15—17, 1757.

Review of *The Prosperity of Britain* . . ., p. 490.
LC, October 18—20, 1757. The one extract is identical in both.

Review of *An Appeal to the Nation* . . ., p. 490.
LC, October 22—25, 1757.

Review of *A Letter to the officers of the British Navy*,
pp. 490–91.
LC, October 25–27, 1757.

Review of *A letter from an officer in the army* . . .,
pp. 492–93.
LC, November 3–5, 1757.

"Ode for his Majesty's Birth-day," pp. 500–01.
LC, November 8–10, 1757. Reprinted verbatim.

LM, II, number XX (November 15 to December 15, 1757).
Published December 17, 1757 (*Daily Advertiser* and *London Chronicle*).
"The Descent, or Peterborough's Ghost," pp. 509–15.
LC, December 20–22, 1757. *LC* deletes first 9 paragraphs;
reprints the rest verbatim, "from the *LM*."

"A Letter from a Gascon Officer . . ." pp. 525–26.
LC, December 1–3, 1757. Reprinted verbatim.

["A Lottery for the Relief of Distressed Virgins"],
pp. 529–30.
LC, November 22–24, 1757. Reprinted verbatim.

"A Journal of the Proceedings of the Doddington East-
Indiaman," pp. 530–39 [and continued in *LM*, III, 25–30.

An "Authentic Narrative" made from this "Journal" was
printed in *LC*, December 31, 1757 –January 3, 1758;
January 3–5, 26–28, 1758.

Prologue to David Garrick's *The Male Coquette*, p. 543.
LC, December 10–13, 1757. Reprinted verbatim.

LM, III (January, 1758). Published February 1, 1758
(*Daily Advertiser*).
"The Poetical Scale," pp. 6–8.
LC, February 4–7, 1758. Reprinted verbatim, "from the
LM."

"Phanor: or the Butterfly Pursuit," pp. 8–11.
LC, February 9–11, 1758. Reprinted verbatim, "from
the *LM*."

Review of Thomas Sheridan's *An Oration* . . ., pp. 30–34.
Reprinted verbatim from *LC*, January 5–7, 1758.

Review of David Garrick's *The Male Coquette*, p. 34.
Prologue printed in *LC*, December 10–13, 1757.
Extracts given in *LC*, December 15–17, 1757.

Prologue and Epilogue to David Garrick's *The Gamesters*,
pp. 37–38.
LC, January 21–24, 1758. Reprinted verbatim.

"Ode, intended for the New Year, 1758. By the late . . .
Colley Cibber," p. 39.
LC, December 31, 1757 — January 3, 1758.
Reprinted verbatim.

LM, III (February, 1758). Published March 1, 1758 (*Daily
Advertiser*).
"Sequel to the Poetical Balance," pp. 59–61.
LC, March 9–11, 1758. Reprinted verbatim, "from the
LM."

Review of J. Z. Holwell's *A Genuine Narrative of the
deplorable Deaths of the English Gentlemen and others,
who were suffocated in the Black Hole in Fort William,
at Calcutta . . .*, pp. 63–69.
LC, February 2–4, 1758. *LM* gives more extracts.

"Mr. Fielding's Plan of a Preservatory and Reformatory,"
pp. 72–74.
LC, February 11–14, 1758. Reprinted verbatim.

Review of John Douglas' *A compleat and Final Detection
of A--d B--r*, pp. 74–78 [and continued on pp. 118–121].
LC, February 28 — March 2, 1758. *LC*'s account is from
the *Critical Review*.

[Thomas Papillon's arguments favoring the importation
of Irish cattle], pp. 80–82.
LC, March 2–4, 1758. Reprinted verbatim, "from the *LM*."

"Register of the Weather in London," p. 83.
LC, March 2–4, 1758. Reprinted verbatim, "from the *LM*."

Two odes from John Home's *Agis*, p. 87.
LC, February 21–23, 1758. Reprinted verbatim.

LM, III (March, 1758). Published April 1, 1758 (*London Chronicle*).
"Of the Scotch Nation. Letter I," pp. 97–101.
Reprinted, with omissions, in *LC*, April 4–6, 1758,
"from the *LM*."

["A candid Examination of the Tragedy of *Agis*"]
pp. 109–13.
Reviewed differently in *LC*, April 4–6, 1758.

[Characters of various persons extracted from Swift's
History of the four last Years of the Queen], pp. 125–28.

Reprinted verbatim from *LC*, March 16—18, 1758, with the character of Walpole, added to fill the column, from *LC*, March 25—28, 1758.

[A letter concerning the habeas corpus bill], pp. 129—30.
Reprinted verbatim from *LC*, March 18—21, 1758.

"Register of the Weather in London," p. 130.
LC, March 30 — April 1, 1758. Reprinted verbatim.

Prologue and Epilogue to John Home's *Agis*, pp. 134—35.
LC, March 2—4, 1758. Reprinted verbatim.

Prologue to Thomas Betterton's *The Amorous Widow, or, the Wanton Wife*, p. 135.
LC, March 11—14, 1758. Reprinted verbatim.

"To Sir John Mordaunt," p. 135.
LC, March 28—30, 1758. Reprinted verbatim.

LM, III (April, 1758). Published May 1, 1758 (*Daily Advertiser*)
"The Writ of Habeas Corpus briefly explained . . ."
pp. 157—60.
LC, April 1—4, 1758. Reprinted verbatim.

"Introduction to a plan for preserving and reforming Young Females, &c. By the Rev. Mr. Dodd," pp. 162—64.
LC, April 20—22, 1758. Reprinted verbatim.

"Mr. Dingley's Proposals for establishing a public place of reception for penitent Prostitutes, &c," pp. 164—68.
LC, April 11—13, 1758. Reprinted verbatim.

Review of Arthur Murphy's *The Upholsterer, or What News?*, pp. 170—73.
LC, April 13—15, 1758.

Review of John Brown's *Estimate of the Manners and Principles of the Times*, Volume II, pp. 173—76.
LC, April 11—13, 1758.

["The humble Petition of Posterity"], p. 176.
LC, May 4—6, 1758. Reprinted verbatim, "from the *LM*."

["Proposals for encouraging of Seamen"], pp. 177—78.
Reprinted verbatim from *LC*, April 15—18, 1758.

The Idler, no. 1, April 15, 1758, pp. 178—79.
LC, April 15—18, 1758.

"Register of the Weather in London," p. 179.
LC, May 4—6, 1758. Reprinted verbatim.

Prologue to Arthur Murphy's *The Upholsterer*, p. 181.
LC, April 13—15, 1758. Reprinted verbatim.

LM, III (May, 1758). Published June 1, 1758 (*Daily Advertiser; London Chronicle*).
"To the Trustees and Managers of Charity-Schools,"
pp. 209—10.
LC, May 13—16, 1758. Reprinted verbatim.

The Monitor, May 6, pp. 210—11.
LC, May 9—11, 1758.

"The Substance of two Letters, on the Cultivation of the
Tea-Shrub, in the British Colonies," pp. 211—12.
The first paragraph is reprinted from *LC*, May 13—16,
1758, and the rest is reprinted from *LC*, May 16—18,
1758.

The Idler, no. 6, May 20, 1758, pp. 212—13.
LC, May 23—25, 1758.

[An extract from Don Antonio de Ulloa's *Voyage to
South America*], pp. 215—16.
A different extract given in *LC*, May 11—13, 1758.

"To the Right Honourable H. B. L. . . .," pp. 216—18.
LC, May 18—20, 1758. Reprinted verbatim.

"A Narrative of the surrender of Vizagapatam . . .,"
pp. 218—21.
LC, May 16—18, 1758. *LM* gives an abridgement, with
slight modifications, of the *LC* account.

Review of *Considerations . . . relative to the Heads of
a Bill for promoting Industry, suppressing Idleness and
Begging . . .*, pp. 221—23.
LC, May 11—13, 1758. Except for the first 13 lines,
LM review is a verbatim reprint of *LC*.

Review of John Armstrong's *Sketches, or Essays on
various subjects*, pp. 227—28.
LC, June 8—10, 1758. Most of the extracts identical in
both.

"Register of the Weather in London," p. 228.
LC, June 1—3, 1758. Reprinted verbatim.

"A Description of London," p. 230.
LC, May 13—16, 1758. Reprinted verbatim.

"Shakespeare Parodied," p. 230.
LC, June 1—3, 1758. Reprinted verbatim.

"An Ode, by the Rev. Mr. Chicken . . .," p. 231.
LC, May 16–18, 1758. Reprinted verbatim.

LM, III (June, 1758). Published July 1, 1758 (*Daily Advertiser*).
"Political Anecdotes, Apothegm and Reflections,"
pp. 248–49.
LC, July 4–6, 1758. Reprinted verbatim, "from the *LM.*"

Review of Saunders Welch's *Proposal to render effectual a Plan, to remove the Nusance of Common Prostitutes from the Streets of this Metropolis . . .*, pp. 254–56.
LC, June 6–8, 1758. Except for some minor variants, especially in the first paragraph, *LM* reprints *LC*.

Review of *A Congratulatory Epistle from a Reformed Rake, to John F---g, Esq; upon the new Scheme of reclaiming Prostitutes*, pp. 256–58.
LC, June 17–20, 1758. *LC* gives more extracts than *LM*.

"Of marking Sheep," by Stephen Hales, p. 258.
LC, June 10–13, 1758. Reprinted verbatim.

"Some Remarks upon a Pamphlet, intitled, *The Conduct of an Admiral*, lately published," pp. 261–62.
Reprinted verbatim from *LC*, June 10–13, 1758.

"To the Printer," p. 264.
Reprinted verbatim from *LC*, June 13–15, 1758.

"Grants for the Year 1758," pp. 266–69.
LC, June 22–24, 1758. Reprinted verbatim.

"An Abstract of the Bill lately passed for the due making of Bread," pp. 269–271.
Given in shortened form in *LC*, July 15–18, 1758.

Extracts from *The Conduct of a noble Commander in America, impartially reviewed . . .*, pp. 273–75.
All these extracts given in the review in *LC*, June 24–27, 1758.

S. Duck's "To Mr. Winter . . .," p. 279.
LC, June 15–17, 1758. Reprinted verbatim.

LM, III (July, 1758). Published August 1, 1758 (*Daily Advertiser*).
["Expedition to France in King William IIId's Reign"],
pp. 301–02.
LC, July 4–6, 1758. Reprinted verbatim.

"A Cure for the Bite of a Viper," p. 302.
LC, June 10–13, 1758. Reprinted verbatim.

"Copy of a Letter from the Earl of Rochester . . .,"
p. 302.
LC, May 18–20, 1758. Reprinted verbatim.

["Abstract of the Bill for the weighing of Hay, &c."],
pp. 302–03.
LC, July 6–8, 1758. Reprinted verbatim.

The Idler, no. 15, July 22, 1758, p. 304.
LC, July 25–27, 1758.

Review of *A Genuine and particular Account of the late
Enterprise on the Coast of France* . . ., pp. 305–07.
LC, July 6–8, 1758.

["Act for encouraging Seamen and paying their Wages"],
pp. 307–10.
Reprinted verbatim from *LC*, July 1–4, 1758.

John Andrew Peyssonels' "Account of a Visitation of the
leprous Persons, in the Isle of Guadaloupe . . .," pp. 310–12.
This whole section given verbatim in *LC*, July 1–4, 1758.
Both *LM* and *LC* take their accounts from *Philosophical
Transactions*, L, Part I, for 1757 (1758), 38–48.

["Custom and Laws compared"], pp. 315–16.
Reprinted verbatim in *LC*, August 1–3, 1758.

The Monitor, July 15, 1758, pp. 316–17.
LC, July 18–20, 1758. *LC* uses slightly different extracts.

["Advantages from political Writing"], pp. 317–19.
Reprinted verbatim from *LC*, July 8–11, 1758.

["Remarkable Particularities discovered on opening a Bee
Hive"], pp. 319–21.
LC, July 6–8, 1758. Reprinted verbatim.

"Some Hints relative to the mending of Roads," pp. 321–22.
Reprinted verbatim from *LC*, June 27–29, 1758, deleting
the first two paragraphs of the *LC* article.

APPENDIX B

Chronological List of Books and Pamphlets

This list presents in order of publication most of the works reviewed in the *Literary Magazine*. In addition various works written, or contributed to, by Johnson and his friends, such as Hawkesworth, Garrick, Burke, Murphy, Mrs. Lennox, and Elizabeth Carter, are included. Some few items are listed without an exact date of publication, and this indicates that they are probably not advertised in the London newspapers examined.

The following abbreviations are used:

DA   *Daily Advertiser*

GEP   *General Evening Post*

Hazen   Allen T. Hazen, *Samuel Johnson's Prefaces & Dedications* (New Haven, 1937)

LC   *London Chronicle*

LEP   *London Evening-Post*

LM   *Literary Magazine: or, Universal Review*

PA   *Public Advertiser*

SM   *Scots Magazine*

Small   Miriam Rossiter Small, *Charlotte Ramsay Lennox* (New Haven, 1935)

Todd   William B. Todd, *A Bibliography of Edmund Burke* (London, 1964)

WEP   *Whitehall Evening Post*

In most instances the dates of publications listed here are earlier than those given by Hazen and Small, in some cases by as much as two months.

The titles of books in this list are kept as short as possible without, I hope, causing any confusion. (A transcription of the title-page of every book Johnson reviewed is given above in Chapter II.)

Subsequent editions of a work are listed directly following the original; subsequent volumes of a work are listed separately.

Work	Date of Publication
Lewis Evans, *Geographical . . . Essays; the first . . . with a map of the Middle British Colonies . . .*	Oct. 22, 1755 (PA; LEP, Oct. 21–23)
Robert Keith, *Catalogue of the Bishops of Scotland*	Edinburgh: Nov. 1755 (SM); and London: June 17, 1756 (LEP)
Robert Whytt, *Physiological Essays . . .*	Edinburgh: Nov. 1755 (SM)
Mrs. Charlotte Lennox, *Memoirs of the Duke of Sully*, 3 v., 4° The Second Edition, 5 v., 8° March 31, 1757 (PA)	Nov. 8, 1755 (PA; WEP, Nov. 6–8)
The Connoisseur, vols. I, II. 12° (2nd edition)	Nov. 25, 1755 (DA; PA)
Francis Home, *Experiments on Bleaching*	Edinburgh: Jan. 1756 (SM); and London: Feb. 11, 1756 (PA)
Samuel Johnson, *Dictionary*, 2 vols., 8°	Jan. 5, 1756 (DA)
William Borlase, *Observations on . . . the Islands of Scilly*	Jan. 20, 1756 (PA; LEP)
William Payne, *Introduction to the Game of Draughts . . .*	Jan. 30, 1756 (DA)
The Rambler, "4th ed.," [sic] 4 vols., 12°	Jan. 30, 1756 (PA)
Thomas Blackwell, *Memoirs of the Court of Augustus*, vol. II	Edinburgh: Feb. 1756 (SM); and London: Feb. 2, 1756 (DA; PA)

The Universal Visiter and Monthly Memorialist, 1st issue	Feb. 2, 1756 (DA; PA)
Stephen Hales, *An Account of a useful Discovery* . . .	Feb. 3, 1756 (PA; WEP, Feb. 3–5).
Richard Rolt, *Dictionary of Trade and Commerce*	Feb. 10, 1756 (WEP, Feb. 7–10)
Thomas Birch, *History of the Royal Society* . . . vols. I, II	Fcb. 12, 1756 (DA; PA)
Jonas Hanway, *A Journal of Eight Days Journey* . . . 1 v., 4° [Several copies signed with this date]	Feb. 28(?), 1756
The Critical Review, I, no. 1	Mar. 1, 1756 (DA; PA)
Mrs. Charlotte Lennox, *Proposals for printing by subscription, A Poetical Dictionary*	Mar. 3, 1756 (DA; not in Small)
Stephen White, *Collateral Bee-Boxes* . . .	Mar. 6, 1756 (WEP, Mar. 4–6)
James Hampton (trans.), *The General History of Polybius*	Mar. 13, 1756 (DA; PA)
Patrick Browne, *The Civil and natural History of Jamaica*	Mar. 18, 1756 (DA; PA)
Sir Thomas Browne, *Christian Morals* (2nd edition)	Mar. 18, 1756 (PA; LEP)
Bourchier Cleeve, *Scheme for preventing a further increase of the National Debt* The Third Edition, Mar. 1, 1757 (LC)	Mar. 26, 1756 (PA; WEP, Mar. 25–27)
Joseph Warton, *An Essay on the Writings and Genius of Pope*	Mar. 26, 1756 (PA; LEP; WEP)

Charles Lucas, *An Essay on Waters*	Apr. 8, 1756 (PA; LEP)
Mrs. Charlotte Lennox, *Memoirs of the Countess of Berci*	Apr. 10, 1756 (PA)
Lewis Evans, *Geographical . . . Essays: the second . . .*	Apr. 13, 1756 (DA)
Arthur Murphy, *The Gray's-Inn Journal*, 2 v.	Apr. 14, 1756 (PA; See LEP, Apr. 10–13, 13–15)
Alexander Russell, *The Natural History of Aleppo*	May 5, 1756 (DA; PA)
Richard Rolt, *A New and Accurate History of South America*	May 6, 1756 (LEP)
A Satirical Review . . . concerning the Earthquake . . . [with] an authentick Account of the late Catastrophe at Lisbon	May 6, 1756 (PA; LEP)
Charles Parkin, *Account of the Invasion under William Duke of Normandy*	May 12, 1756 (DA; PA)
Sir Isaac Newton, *Four Letters from Sir Isaac Newton to Dr. Bentley*	May 12, 1756 (PA; LEP)
Literary Magazine, I, no. I	May 15, 1756 (DA; LEP)
Edmund Burke, *A Vindication of Natural Society . . .* The Second Edition, with a new Preface Dec. 17, 1757 (LEP; LC; PA; Todd, p. 26)	May 18, 1756 (PA)
Peter Whalley (ed.), *The Works of Ben Jonson*	June 4, 1756 (PA)
John Armstrong, *History of the Island of Minorca*, 2d ed.	June 5, 1756 (PA)
The Second Part of The Satirical Review . . . [See May 6, 1756]	June 5, 1756 (PA)

John George Keysler, *Travels through*   June 5, 1756 (PA)
   Germany . . . vol. I, 4°

Samuel Johnson, *Proposals for printing*   June 8, 1756 (LEP)
   by subscription, The Dramatick
   Works of William Shakespeare

Literary Magazine, I, no. II   June 15, 1756 (PA)

John Douglas, *Six Letters from*   June 28, 1756 (PA; WEP,
   A---d B---r to Father Sheldon . . .   June 26–29)

Archibald Bower, *Mr. Archibald Bower's*   July 1, 1756 (DA)
   Affidavit in Answer to the False
   Accusation brought against him by
   Papists

Philosophical Transactions, Vol. XLIX.   July 6, 1756 (DA)
   Part I for 1755

John Free, *A Sermon preached at*   July 8, 1756 (DA)
   St. John's, 29 May 1756

Dr. Hoadly and Mr. Wilson, *Observa-*   July 13, 1756 (PA)
   tions on . . . *Electrical Experiments*

Literary Magazine, I, no. III   July 15, 1756 (PA)

An Account of the Conferences held,   July 24, 1756 (DA)
   and Treaties made . . . [Sabin
   36337; Church 1010]

R. Lovett, *The Subtil Medium proved* . . .   July 24, 1756 (DA)

[Bourchier Cleeve?], *Bower Vindicated*   August 11, 1756 (PA)
   from the False Insinuations and
   Accusations of the Papists

Literary Magazine, I, no. IV [N.B.   Aug. 16, 1756 (DA; PA)
   Aug. 15 was a Sunday]

Literary Magazine, I, no. V   Sept. 15, 1756 (PA)

A Letter to a Member of Parliament in the Country . . .	Oct. 2, 1756 (DA; PA; LEP)
John Shebbeare, *An Appeal to the People* . . . *Part the First*	Oct. 7, 1756 (PA; LEP; GEP)
Samuel Bever, *The Cadet, A Military Treatise*	Oct. 9, 1756 (DA; PA; GEP)
Literary Magazine, I, no. VI	Oct. 15, 1756 (DA; PA)
The Monitor, vol. I, 8°	Oct. 16, 1756 (LEP)
James Lind, *A Treatise on the Scurvy* . . . 2nd ed.	Oct. 17, 1756 (PA)
Some further Particulars in Relation to the Case of Admiral Byng	Oct. 27, 1756 (DA; PA)
David Mallet, *The Conduct of the Ministry impartially examined* The Second Edition, Nov. 11, 1756 (PA; GEP)	Oct. 30, 1756 (DA; PA; LEP)
The Test, 1st number	Nov. 6, 1756 (DA; PA)
Literary Magazine, I, no. VII	Nov. 15, 1756 (PA)
Ten Precepts written by Lord Burghley	[Nov. (?), 1756]
The Con-Test, 1st number	Nov. 23, 1756 (PA)
Adam Ferguson, *Reflections previous to the establishment of a Militia*	Nov. 25, 1756 (PA)
Claude du Choisel, *Method of treating persons bit by mad animals*	Nov. 30, 1756 (DA)
Giuseppe Baretti, *The Italian Library*	Dec. 8, 1756 (PA)
The Adventurer, 3rd ed., 4 vols.	Dec. 9, 1756 (PA; GEP)
Literary Magazine, I, no. VIII	Dec. 16, 1756 (PA; GEP)

The London Chronicle, 1st number (e.g., see advertisement in DA, Nov. 22, 1756)   Jan. 1, 1757

Thomas Francklin, *Translation, A Poem* 2nd ed.   Jan. 3, 1757 (DA; PA)

John Douglas, *Bower and Tillemont compared* . . .   Jan. 6, 1757 (PA; GEP, Jan. 1–4, 4–6)

Archibald Bower, *Mr. Bower's Answer to a Scurrilous Pamphlet* . . . Part I   Jan. 6, 1757 (DA; PA; GEP)

The Protest   Jan. 14, 1757 (DA; PA)

Literary Magazine, I, no. IX   Jan. 20, 1757 (GEP)

Archibald Bower, *Mr. Bower's Answer to a New Charge brought against him* . . .   Jan. 22, 1757 (DA; LC; WEP)

Tobias Smollett, *The Reprisal, or, The Tars of Old England*   Feb. 1, 1757 (DA; PA; LC; LEP)

William Whitehead, *Elegies, with an Ode to the Tiber*   Feb. 4, 1757 (PA; GEP; LEP)

Elizabeth Harrison, *Miscellanies on Moral and Religious Subjects*   Feb. 4, 1757 (PA)

David Hume, *Four Dissertations*   Feb. 5, 1757 (GEP)

Archibald Bower, *The Second Part of Mr. Bower's Answer to a Scurrilous Pamphlet* . . .   Feb. 10, 1757 (PA; WEP)

Thomas Birch, *History of the Royal Society* . . . vols. III, IV   Feb. 10, 1757 (DA; PA)

Literary Magazine, II, no. X   Feb. 17, 1757 (DA; LC; GEP)

Samuel Foote, *The Author, a Comedy*   Feb. 17, 1757 (DA; PA)

The Connoisseur, vols. III, IV. 12° (2nd ed.) The Third Edition, 4 vols., 12°, Dec. 12, 1757 (DA)	Feb. 22, 1757 (DA; PA; LEP)
John Douglas, *A Full Confutation of all the Facts advanced in Mr. Bower's Three Defences* . . .	Mar. 12, 1757 (PA)
Mrs. Charlotte Lennox (trans.), *Memoirs for the History of Mme. de Maintenon*	Mar. 12, 1757 (DA; PA)
John Dyer, *The Fleece: a Poem*	Mar. 15, 1757 (PA; LC; LEP)
A Supplement to the Works of Alexander Pope	Mar. 15, 1757 (PA; LEP)
John Gilbert Cooper, *Letters concerning Taste* . . . 3rd ed.	Mar. 15, 1757 (LEP)
Literary Magazine, II, no. XI	Mar. 16, 1757 (PA)
Jonas Hanway, *A Morning's Thoughts on Reading the Test and Contest*	Mar. 19, 1757 (PA; LC; GEP)
John Home, *Douglas, a Tragedy* (1st London ed.)	Mar. 19, 1757 (DA; PA; LEP)
Memoirs of the Marquis of Torcy . . . 2 v.	Mar. 22, 1757 (PA; See GEP, Mar. 17—19; GEP & LEP, Mar. 19—22)
William Chambers, *Designs of Chinese Buildings* . . .	Mar. 28, 1757 (PA)
A Letter to a Gentleman in the Country . . . *Giving an authentic* . . . *Account of the Confinement, Behaviour, and Death of Admiral Byng*	Mar. 29, 1757 (DA)
Soame Jenyns, *A Free Inquiry into the Nature and Origin of Evil* The Second Edition, May 31, 1757 (DA; PA)	Mar. 30, 1757 (PA)

The Third Edition, "revised and
amended" Apr. 20, 1758 (PA; WEP)

John Brown, *An Estimate of the Manners* Mar. 31, 1757 (PA)
   and Principles of the Times
   The Second Edition, Apr. 14, 1757
     (LEP)
   The Third Edition, May 5, 1757 (LEP)
   The Fourth Edition, May 31, 1757 (DA)
   The Fifth Edition, July 4, 1757 (PA)
   The Sixth Edition, Sept. 1, 1757 (DA)
   The Seventh Edition, Apr. 20, 1758
     (LC; WEP)

[Edmund Burke], *An Account of the* Apr. 1, 1757 (DA)
   European Settlements in America
   ... 2 vols., 8°
   The Second Edition [2 v., dated 1758],
    Nov. 24, 1757 (DA; Todd, p. 30)

Field Marshal Count Saxe, *Reveries; or,* Apr. 7, 1757 (DA; PA)
   Memoirs upon the Art of War

Elizabeth Carter, *Proposals for printing* Apr. 14, 1757 (PA; GEP;
   by subscription, All the Works of LEP)
   Epictetus

The Rev. John Lindsay, *The Evangelical* Apr. 16, 1757 (PA)
   History ... Harmonized

Literary Magazine, II, no. XII Apr. 16, 1757 (PA)

Edmund Burke, *A philosophical Enquiry* Apr. 21, 1757 (DA;
   into the Origin of our Ideas of the PA; LC; GEP; LEP)
   Sublime and Beautiful

Robert Wood, *The Ruins of Balbec* Apr. 21, 1757 (DA; PA;
    GEP; LEP)

John Shebbeare, *An Appeal to the* Apr. 22, 1757 (PA)
   People ... Part the Second

Jonas Hanway, *A Journal of Eight Days Journey* . . . 2nd ed., 2 vols., 8°

Apr. 27, 1757 (PA; See LEP & WEP, Apr. 23–26; WEP, Apr. 26–28)

James Lind, *On Preserving the health of seamen in the Navy*

Apr. 28, 1757 (PA; GEP)

William Wilkie, *The Epigoniad*

The Second Edition, "carefully corrected and improved"

Edinburgh: May, 1757 (SM); London: June 25, 1757 (PA) Mar. 29, 1759 (LC)

Literary Magazine, II, no. XIII

May 17, 1757 (PA; LC; GEP)

Horace Walpole, *A Letter from Xo Ho, a Chinese Philosopher*
The Second Edition, May 20, 1757 (DA)
The Third Edition, May 24, 1757 (DA)
The Fourth Edition, May 31, 1757 (PA; LEP)
The Fifth Edition, June 14, 1757 (PA)

May 18, 1757 (PA; LEP, May 17–19)

Familiar Letters of Dr. William Sancroft . . .

May 19, 1757 (DA; PA; LEP)

Medical Observations and Inquiries. By a Society of Physicians in London

May 23, 1757 (PA)

Robert Bolton, *The Ghost of Ernest*

May 31, 1757 (GEP)

Daniel Peter Layard, *On contagious distemper among horned cattle* . . .

June 1, 1757 (DA; PA)

Literary Magazine, II, no. XIV

June 17, 1757 (PA)

"A Reply to a Paper in the Gazetteer of May 26, 1757"

June 17, 1757 (in LM, no. 14)

Archibald Bower, *Mr. Bower's Reply*   June 24, 1757 (DA; PA)
   to a Scurrilous Libel . . . [Douglas'
   Full Confutation]

Thomas Gataker, *Internal Use of Solanum*   June 28, 1757 (LC)
   or Night-shade
   The Second Edition, July 21, 1757
    (PA; LC)
   The Fourth Edition, Oct. 27, 1757
    (LC)
   The Fifth Edition, Dec. 14, 1757
    (PA)

Literary Magazine, II, no. XV   July 19, 1757 (PA)

A. Henderson (trans.), *Memoirs of*   Aug. 4, 1757 (PA; LEP)
   Field Marshal Leopold Count Daun

Henry Saxby, *The British Customs*   Aug. 4, 1757 (PA)

Thomas Gray, *Odes*   Aug. 8, 1757 (DA; PA)

Literary Magazine, II, no. XVI   Aug. 16, 1757 (LC)

The Monitor, vol. II, 8°   Aug. 25, 1757 (PA; LEP)

A full Answer to an infamous Libel,   Sept. 5, 1757 (DA; PA)
   intitled, A Letter to the Right
   Honourable Lord B---y

The Herald: or, Patriot Proclaimer,   Sept. 17, 1757 (PA; LC;
   1st number   LEP)

Literary Magazine, II, no. XVII   Sept. 20, 1757 (LC)

A Genuine Account of the late grand   Oct. 10, 1757 (DA; PA)
   Expedition to the Coast of France
   under . . . Admirals Hawke [etc.]
   The Second Edition, Oct. 14, 1757
    (PA)

The Prosperity of Britain . . .   Oct. 11, 1757 (PA; LEP)

Paul Hentzner, *A Journey into*   Oct. 17, 1757
England in 1598 (See *Journal of the*
Printing Office at Strawberry Hill
[1923 ed.], p. 5)

Literary Magazine, II, no. XVIII   Oct. 18, 1757 (DA; LC)

Literary Magazine, II, no. XIX   Nov. 19, 1757 (LC)

Mrs. Charlotte Lennox, *Philander*   Dec. 3, 1757 (LEP)

David Garrick, *The Male Coquette, or*   Dec. 12, 1757 (PA)
MDCCLVII. A Farce in Two Acts

Literary Magazine, II, no. XX   Dec. 17, 1757 (DA; LC)

Thomas Sheridan, *An Oration* [given in   Jan. 4, 1758 (DA)
Dublin, Dec. 6, 1757]

J. Z. Holwell, *A Genuine Narrative of*   Jan. 27, 1758 (PA; WEP,
the Deplorable Deaths of the English   Jan. 24–26, 26–28)
Gentlemen . . . [in the Black Hole of
Calcutta]

Mrs. Charlotte Lennox, *The History of*   Jan. 28, 1758 (PA; WEP)
Henrietta

James Bennet, *Proposals for printing by*   Jan. 28, 1758 (PA)
subscription the English Works of
Roger Ascham

Literary Magazine, III (for Jan., 1758)   Feb. 1, 1758 (DA; PA)

John Corpe, *Some Very Remarkable*   Feb. 4, 1758 (WEP)
Facts, lately discovered, relating to
the Conduct of the Jesuits, with
regard to Mr. Bower . . .
The Second Edition, "with Preface
and Postscript" Apr. 18, 1758 (DA)

William Arnold, *Mr. A---d's Motives for*   Feb. 13, 1758 (DA; PA)
Renouncing the Popish, and Re-
embracing the Protestant Religion

Archibald Bower, *One very remarkable*   Feb. 15, 1758 (DA)
Fact more, relating to the Conduct
of the Jesuits . . .

John Douglas, *A Complete and Final*   Feb. 23, 1758 (PA)
Detection of A---d B---r . . .

Literary Magazine, III (for Feb., 1758)   Mar. 1, 1758 (DA)

John Home, *Agis: A Tragedy*   Mar. 2, 1758 (DA; PA;
                                                WEP)

Robert Wallace, *Characteristics of the*   Mar. 11, 1758 (DA; PA;
Present Political State of Great   LEP; WEP)
Britain
The Second Edition, July 13, 1758
    (DA; PA; LEP)

William Blackstone, *Considerations on*   Mar. 14, 1758 (PA; LEP)
the Question, Whether Tenants by
Copy of Court Roll . . . are Freeholders
qualified to vote

Jonathan Swift, *The History of the Four*   Mar. 17, 1758 (DA; PA;
Last Years of the Queen   also see LC, LEP, and
                                                WEP of Mar. 16—18)

R. Dodsley, *A Collection of Poems . . .*   Mar. 18, 1758 (LEP;
by Several Hands Volumes V, VI   WEP)

Literary Magazine, III (for Mar., 1758)   Apr. 1, 1758 (LC)

Temple Henry Croker, *Bower detected*   Apr. 5, 1758 (PA)
as an Historian . . .

A Proposal for the Encouragement of   Apr. 6, 1758 (LEP; WEP)
Seamen to serve more readily . . .

The Universal Chronicle, 1st number   Apr. 8, 1758

John Brown, *An Estimate of the Manners*   Apr. 8, 1758 (LC)
and Principles of the Times, vol. II

George Crine, *The Management of the*   Apr. 10, 1758 (PA)
  Gout [with Bardana] . . .
  The Second Edition, Apr. 20, 1758
    (WEP)
  The Third Edition, May 9, 1758
    (PA)
  The Fourth Edition, July 1, 1758
    (PA)
  The Fifth Edition, July 27, 1758
    (PA)

Arthur Murphy, *The Upholsterer, or,*   Apr. 12, 1758 (PA; LEP,
  What News? A Farce, in Two Acts   Apr. 8–11; WEP, Apr.
                                              11–13)

Don George Juan and Don Antonio de   Apr. 14, 1758 (PA; WEP)
  Ulloa, *A Voyage to South America*,
  2 v., 8°

The Idler, number 1   Apr. 15, 1758 (in
                                              Universal Chronicle)

Elizabeth Carter (trans.), *The Works of*   Apr. 17, 1758 (PA; See
  Epictetus, 4°   WEP, Mar. 21–23; LEP,
                                              Apr. 15–18)

The Herald; or, Patriot Proclaimer . . .   Apr. 27, 1758 (PA; WEP)
  2 vols., 12°

Literary Magazine, III (for Apr., 1758)   May 1, 1758 (DA)

Letters to the Estimator of the Manners   May 2, 1758 (PA; WEP)
  and Principles of the Times. By One
  who has served the State
  The Second Edition, May 10, 1758
    (DA)

John Brown (ed.), *The Power of*   May 4, 1758 (WEP)
  Protestant Religious Principle . . .
  Exemplified in a Diary of the Siege
  of Londonderry, by the Rev. George
  Walker

William Bailey, *A Treatise on the*   May 4, 1758 (WEP)
  Better Employment . . . of the
  Poor in Workhouses

The Conduct of Admiral Knowles . . .   May 8, 1758 (DA; PA;
  set in a true light . . .   LEP, May 7–9)
  The Second Edition, "Corrected and
    Amended" May 20, 1758 (LEP;
    WEP)

Some Doubts, occasioned by the Second   May 11, 1758 (DA)
  Volume of an Estimate of the Manners
  and Principles of the Times. Humbly
  proposed to the Author, or to the
  Public
  The Second Edition, July 20, 1758
    (DA)

Saunders Welch, *A Proposal to render*   May 22, 1758 (DA; PA)
  effectual a Plan, to remove the
  Nuisance of Common Prostitutes
  from the Streets

John Armstrong, *Sketches; or, Essays*   May 23, 1758 (DA; PA;
  on Various Subjects . . . by Launcelot   WEP)
  Temple
  The Second Edition, corrected.
    June 30, 1758 (PA)

A Congratulatory Epistle from   May 25, 1758 (DA; PA)
  a Reformed Rake, to John F------g,
  Esq; upon the new Scheme of
  reclaiming Prostitutes . . .
  The Second Edition, July 11, 1758
    (PA)

Robert Lowth, *The Life of William of*   May 27, 1758 (DA; PA;
  Wykeham . . .   LC; LEP; WEP)

William Borlase, *The Natural History*   May 29, 1758 (DA; WEP,
  of Cornwall   May 25–27, 27–30)

Literary Magazine, III (for May, 1758)   June 1, 1758 (DA; PA)

John Brown, *An Explanatory Defence of the Estimate of the Manners and Principles of the Times*	June 19, 1758 (DA)
Literary Magazine, III (for June, 1758)	July 1, 1758 (DA)
A Genuine and Particular Account of the Late Enterprize on the Coast of France . . .	July 7, 1758 (DA; PA; LEP, July 6–8)
Literary Magazine, III (for July, 1758)	Aug. 1, 1758 (DA)

INDEX

Names of authors are followed by the titles of the works most frequently cited in this book; however, the entries also list in the same sequence all other references to the author. If a work is cited in the text only by title, entries are usually listed under both title and author (if known).

Since a discussion of the book trade (and the imprints of books) provided more than seventy names of persons and firms, I have listed in a separate category all "Printers, Publishers, and Booksellers." It seemed convenient and helpful to provide such a separate listing, although I may be in error in excluding certain names from the list. For example, so far as I know Griffith Jones was only an author and editor (as well as owning shares in some periodical publications), so his name is listed only in the main index. If in doubt, please check both places.

For those of bibliographical interests, I have also provided a special category of "Bibliographica" which lists details of printing and publishing the books described in Chapter II.

Account of the Conferences held, and Treaties made . . ., An, 102, 131
Adventurer, The, 4, 59, 132
Akenside, Mark, 8, 98
Ames, Joseph, 102
Appeal to the People, An, see: Shebbeare, John
Armstrong, John, *The History of the Island of Minorca,* 19, 29, 33–35, 82, 130
Armstrong, John, *Sketches, or Essays on various subjects,* 124, 141
Arnold, William, 138
Ascham, Roger, 138

Bacon, Francis, 36
Bailey, William, 141
Balderston, Katharine C., 104

Baretti, Giuseppe, 81, 132
Bate, Walter Jackson, 4, 99
Bedingfeld, Sir Henry, 45
Bee, The (by Oliver Goldsmith), 3
Bennet, James, 138
Bentley, Richard, 43
Betterton, Thomas, 123
Bever, Samuel, *The Cadet,* 17, 31, 67, 85, 132
Bibliographica (listed by item no. in Chapter II)
  Binding. Jonas Hanway, no. 37; Thomas Hollis, no. 38 (4th ed.).
  Bowyer, William, books printed by, no. 1 (2d ed., 1756), and no. 18.
  Cancels, unusual printing of, no. 37.
  Editions, no priority established, no. 25; priority now established, no. 38; not published, no. 27.

Bibliographica (contd.)
Fine-paper copies, nos. 18 and 23.
Parts, publication in, no. 21
Press figures.
Three per gathering without cancels, nos. 15, 21, 27.
Unusual use of, no. 23; also, see note under "press figures" in no. 24.
Proposals for forthcoming edition, nos. 17 and 21.
Publisher's contract, no. 6.
Reissue.
Additional material added, nos. 1, 3, 6, 8, 15, 18.
Cancel title, no. 4.
Reprints, inexpensive ones, by same publisher, nos. 25, 26, 30.
Strahan, William, books printed by, nos. 3 (v. 1 and 3 only), 8, 16, 22, 30, and 38 (ed. 1—4).
Subscription edition, nos. 18, 23; see nos. 17 and 21, which had proposals but no list of subscribers.
Title. Misdated, no. 8; Variant, nos. 24 and 30.
Birch, Thomas, *The History of the Royal Society*, 16, 29, 36—38, 80, 81, 82, 84, 116, 129, 133
Blackstone, William, 139
Blackwell, Thomas, *Memoirs of the Court of Augustus*, 16, 30, 41—42, 86, 128
Bloom, Edward A., x, 18, 99, 107, 108, 109, 112
Bolton, Robert, 136
Booth, John, 102
Borlase, William, *Observations on . . . the Islands of Scilly*, 16, 30, 43—44, 82, 88, 128, 141
Boswell, James, 6, 13, 15, 16, 17, 18, 83—84, 97, 99, 103, 109, 112
Bower, Archibald,
Affidavit, 19, 20, 30, 45—46, 131; *Answer to a scurrilous Pamphlet*, 20—22, 31, 70, 81, 82, 114, 133, 137, 138, 139.
Also see entries under: Douglas, John.
British Magazine, 3, 95

Brown, John (1715—1766), including replies to his *Estimate*, 116, 120, 123, 135, 137, 139, 140, 141, 142
Browne, Patrick, *The Civil and Natural History of Jamaica*, 17, 30, 51—53, 82, 84, 129
Browne, Sir Thomas, *Christian Morals* (1756), 4, 9, 17, 30, 46—47, 81, 99, 129
Brutus, 86
Burghley, Lord, 132
Burke, Edmund, 2, 82, 83, 100, 117, 127, 130, 135
Burney, Charles, 9, 15, 100, 101
Burney, Mrs. Charles, 15
Butler, James A., "Samuel Johnson: Defender of Admiral Byng" (1969), 69
Byng, Admiral John (d. 1757), 10, 17, 27—28, 31, 33, 63, 64, 67, 68, 69, 72, 82, 87, 114, 115, 117, 132, 134

Caesar, Augustus, 115
Carter, Elizabeth, 81, 127, 135, 140
Carteret, Father, 21
Centinel, The, 112, 115
Chalmers, Alexander, 15
Chambers, Robert, of Lincoln College, Oxford, 2, 7
Chambers, William, 118, 134
Chapman, R. W., 95, 98, 99, 100, 103, 104
Charles XII (of Sweden), 19, 56
Chesterfield, Earl of, 49
Chicken, Mr., 125
Chishull, Edmund, 118
Choisel, Claude du, 115, 132
Cibber, Colley, 26, 114, 122
Cibber, Theophilus, 119
Cicero, 53
Citizen of the World (by Oliver Goldsmith), 8
Cleeve, Bourchier, 102, 113, 129, 131
Cochrane, J. A., 96
Cock-Lane ghost, 22
Conduct of Admiral Knowles . . ., *The*, 141
Conduct of the Ministry Impartially Examined, The, see: Mallet, David
Connoisseur, The, 82, 112, 115, 128, 134

Con-Test, The, 14, 23—24, 31, 71—72,
   84, 112, 114, 132, 134
Cooper, John Gilbert, 134
Courtney, William Prideaux, x, 16,
   18, 99
Corpe, John, 138
Crane, Ronald S., 102
Crine, George, 140
Critical Review, 2, 19, 79, 80, 101,
   109, 112, 129
Crokcr, John Wilson, 15
Croker, Temple Henry, 139
Cumberland, Duke of, 67

Daily Courant, 1
Damien, Robert Francis, 114
Daun, Field Marshal Leopold
   Count, 137
Dictionary . . . (by Samuel Johnson),
   5, 8, 94, 104, 105, 128
Dingley, Mr., 123
Dodd, William, 123
Douglas, John,
   Six Letters from A--d B--r, 19, 20,
   30, 44—45, 131;
   Bower and Tillemont compared . . .
   20—22, 31, 69—70, 81, 122, 133,
   134, 139.
   Also see entries under: Bower,
   Archibald.
Drummond, Alexander, 42
Duck, Stephen, 125
Dyer, John, The Fleece, 82, 116,
   134

Eloisa to Abelard (by Pope), 26, 89
Epictetus, 81, 135, 140
European Magazine, 9, 17, 65, 99
Evans, Lewis, Geographical, Historical,
   Political, Philosophical and Mechani-
   cal Essays. The First . . . (1755), 10,
   17, 30, 59—62, 85, 128, 130

Ferguson, Adam, 132
Fielding, John, 122, 125, 141
Fifth Letter to the People of England,
   A (by John Shebbeare), 65
Foote, Samuel, 115, 133
Fordyce, John, 112
Fothergill, Dr., 112
Foundling Hospital, 11—14

Fox, Henry, 23, 31, 71
Francis, Philip, 23, 31, 71
Francklin, Thomas, 19, 82, 101, 133
Free, John, 102, 131
Friedman, Arthur, 98, 99
Full Answer to an infamous Libel . . .,
   A, 119, 137

Garrick, David, 120, 121, 122, 127, 138
Gataker, Thomas, 119, 137
Gazette, The, 64
Gazetteer, The, 12—14, 78, 100, 101,
   136
Gentleman's Magazine, 1, 10, 11, 16,
   17, 101, 103, 107, 109, 112
Genuine Account of the late Grand
   Expedition . . ., A, 120, 137
Genuine and Particular Account of
   the late Enterprize on the Coast of
   France, A, 126, 142
Gipson, Lawrence Henry, 60
Gleig, George, 16, 17, 18
Goldsmith, Oliver, 3, 5, 8, 98, 99, 102
Goodwin, Gordon, 95
Gordan, John D., 100
Gray, Thomas, 120, 137
Gray's-Inn Journal, The, 3, 16, 29, 38—
   39, 81, 82, 84, 130
Greene, Donald J., x, 7, 9, 10, 15, 16,
   17, 18, 19, 20, 22, 62, 99, 100, 101,
   102, 105, 107, 112
Grey, Mr., 84

Haig, Robert, 78
Haight, Gordon, 104
Hales, Stephen, An Account of
   a Useful Discovery . . ., 17, 30, 47—
   48, 84, 117, 125, 129
Hamilton, William Gerard, 93
Hampton, James (translator of the
   General History of Polybius), 16, 29,
   40—41, 81, 82, 129
Hanway, Jonas (including all references
   to both editions of his Journal of
   Eight Days Journey . . .), 11, 12, 14,
   15, 17, 18, 31, 32, 65—67, 73—75,
   78, 85, 92, 101, 117, 129, 134, 136
Harrison, Elizabeth, Miscellanies, 17,
   30, 58—59, 80, 81, 84, 133
Hawkesworth, John, 4, 59, 103, 127
Hawkins, John, 2, 6, 8, 16, 17, 95, 99

Hazen, Allen T., 5, 15, 16, 18, 95, 98, 99, 104, 107, 108, 109, 111, 113, 127
Hemlow, Joyce, 100
Henderson, A., 137
Hentzner, Paul, 138
Herald; or, Patriot Proclaimer, The, 3, 97, 112, 137, 140
Hill, George Birkbeck, x, 15, 95
Histoire et les Mémoires de l'Académie Royale des Sciences, 109, 112
Hoadly, Dr., 102, 131
Holwell, John Zephaniah, 122, 138
Home, Francis, Experiments on Bleaching, 16, 30, 46, 82, 128
Home, John, Douglas, 82, 116, 117, 122, 123, 134, 139
Horace, 67, 115
Hoyles, Mrs., 22
Humanist, The, 112
Hume, David, Four Dissertations, 82, 83, 115, 116, 133

Idler, The (by Samuel Johnson), 7, 112, 113, 123, 124, 126, 140
Isham, Ralph, 97
Isles, Duncan E., 100

Jenyns, Soame, A Free Inquiry into the Nature and Origin of Evil, 9, 17, 31, 75−78, 88, 90−93, 100, 105, 117, 134, 135;
Short but serious Reasons for a National Militia, 116
Johnson, Samuel.
Contributions to Literary Magazine: book reviews, 15−28; writings other than reviews, 6−7. Nature and duration of Johnson's association with the LM, 6−15. Description of books S.J. reviewed in LM, 29−78. S.J.'s techniques as a reviewer, 79−94. Major works not printed in LM: Dictionary, 5, 8, 94, 104, 105, 128; Idler, 7, 112, 113, 123, 124, 126, 140; Life of Akenside, 101; Congreve, 26, 101; Dr. Francis Cheynel, 4; Gray, 101; Pope, 26, 90, 105; West, 101. New Prologue . . . to Comus, 4; Rambler, 3, 4, 8, 128; Rasselas, 5, 104; Shakespeare (S.J.'s ed. of), 5, 7,

Johnson, Samuel (contd.) 15, 80, 100, 117, 131. Johnson's prefaces and dedications are listed under the authors of the books.
Johnson, Sir William, 102
Jones, Griffith, 2, 3, 6, 95, 97, 98
Jonson, Ben, 102, 130

Keith, Robert, A Large new Catalogue of the Bishops . . . of Scotland, 17, 30, 50−51, 85, 128
Keysler, John George, see: Keyssler, Johann Georg
Keyssler, Johann Georg, Travels through Germany, 18, 19, 30, 54−56, 85, 131
King's Head, in Ivy Lane, 2
Kolb, Gwin J., 98
Krutch, Joseph Wood, 105

Lady's Magazine, The, 3
Lauder, William, Essay on Milton's Use and Imitation of the Moderns . . ., 4, 9, 22
Law, William, 104
Layard, Daniel Peter, 118, 136
Leighton, Robert, 85
Lennox, Mrs. Charlotte, translator of Memoirs of . . . the Duke of Sully, 10, 17, 18, 30, 56−58, 79, 80, 81, 84, 127, 128, 129, 130, 134, 138
"Letter from an Officer at Minorca" (dated Feb. 27, 1756), 19, 34−35
Letter to a Gentleman in the Country . . . Giving an authentick and circumstantial Account of the Confinement, Behaviour, and Death of Admiral Byng, 27−28, 31, 72−73, 116, 134
Letter to a Member of Parliament in the Country . . . relative to the Case of Admiral Byng, 17, 31, 63−64, 132
Liebert, Herman W., 99
"Life of Akenside" (by Samuel Johnson), 101
"Life of Congreve" (by Samuel Johnson), 26, 101
"Life of Dr. Francis Cheynel" (by Samuel Johnson) in The Student (1751), 4
"Life of Gray" (by Samuel Johnson), 101

"Life of Pope" (by Samuel Johnson), 26, 90, 105
"Life of West" (by Samuel Johnson), 101
Lind, James, 118, 132, 136
Lindsay, The Rev. John, *Evangelical History of our Lord Jesus Christ . . .* (1757), 4–5, 18, 117, 135
Literary Magazine: or, Universal Review, The. Founding the magazine, 2–3; Johnson's contributions, 6–28; printers, editors and publishers of, 2–5, 107–109; reliance on the *London Chronicle*, see Appendix A. For a bibliographical description of the magazine, see the introduction to volume I of the Garland facsimile reprint.
Lives of the English Poets (by Samuel Johnson), 101
Lloyd's Evening Post, 3, 14, 97, 98
London Chronicle, The. There are scores of references to this work; see especially the Preface, Chapter I, Notes to Chapter I (esp. n. 12), and Appendix A.
Lovejoy, Arthur O., 105
Lovett, R., 102, 131
Lowth, Robert, 141
Lucan, 41
Lucas, Charles, *An Essay on Waters*, 17, 30, 48–50, 130
Lyttelton, Charles, 44

Macclesfield, Earl of, 48
McClure, Ruth K., 12–14, 100
McKillop, Alan Dugald, 101
Mallet, David, *The Conduct of the Ministry Impartially Examined*, 17, 31, 68–69, 132
Malone, Edmond, 15, 16, 93, 105
Medical Observations and Enquiries, by a Society of Physicians in London (1757), 109, 119, 136
"Memoirs of the King of Prussia" (by Samuel Johnson), 7, 114
Memoirs of the Marquis of Torcy, 116, 134
Miller, C. William, *Benjamin Franklin's Philadelphia Printing . . .* (1974), 60, 62

Milton, John, 4, 22
Mirgehan, 39
Miscellaneous Pieces (by Soame Jenyns), 78
Monarch, HMS, 27, 28
Monitor, The, 112, 116, 119, 120, 124, 126, 132, 137
Monthly Review, 1–2, 8, 19, 79, 80, 95, 96, 98, 100, 103, 109, 112
Mordaunt, Sir John, 123
Murphy, Arthur, xiii–xiv, 2, 3, 6, 9, 16, 22, 23, 26, 29, 31, 38, 71, 81, 82, 84, 95, 96, 98, 100, 123, 124, 127, 130, 140
Museum, The, 8, 98

Nangle, Benjamin Christie, 95
Needham, Dr., 84
Newcastle, Thomas Pelham-Holles, Duke of, 9, 10
Newnham, Lord, 26
New Prologue . . . at the Presentation of Comus . . . A (by Samuel Johnson), 4
Newton, A. Edward, 103
Newton, Sir Isaac, *Four Letters from Sir Isaac Newton to Doctor Bentley . . .*, 16, 30, 43, 130
Nichol Smith, David, x, 18, 23, 109, 113
Normandy, William, Duke of, 53

Offarel, Richard, 33
Osborn, James M., 100
Ovid, 64

Papillon, Thomas, 122
Parkin, Charles, *An Impartial Account of the Invasion under William Duke of Normandy*, 18, 30, 53–54, 85, 130
Patkul, Johann Reinhold, 19, 56
Payne, William, 81, 128
Percy, Thomas, 8
Peyssonels, John Andrew, 126
Philosophical Enquiry into the Origin of our Ideas of the Sublime and Beautiful, A (by Edmund Burke), reviewed by Arthur Murphy, 2, 82, 83, 100, 117, 135
Philosophical Transactions, 17, 30, 54, 84, 109, 112, 119, 126, 131
Piggott, Stuart, 99

Pitt, William, 10, 23
Plantagenet, Richard, 114
Plumptre, Mr., 12
"Poetical Scale," 9, 121
Polybius, 16, 29, 40, 41, 129
Pope, Alexander, 26, 38, 39, 88—90,
    93, 105, 134
Pope, Dudley, *At 12 Mr Byng was shot*
    (1962), 68
Powell, L. F., x, 15
Prefaces, Biographical and Critical, to
    the Works of the English Poets
    (by Samuel Johnson), 105
Printers, Publishers and Booksellers
    Allen, Edmund, 8
    Baldwin, Robert, 2, 44
    Baskerville, John, 81
    Bladon, Samuel, 68, 69
    Bouquet, J., 4
    Bowyer, William, 34, 35, 52, 96, 97,
        98
    Buckland, James, 58
    Buckley, Samuel, 1
    Cadell, Thomas, 5
    Carnan, Thomas, 5
    Cave, Edward, 1, 11
    Clements, Richard, 44
    Collins, Benjamin, 3, 5, 96, 97, 98
    Cooke, John, 63, 65
    Cooper, Mary, 39
    Corbett, Charles (junior), 71
    Davies, Thomas, 16, 17
    Davis, Charles, 33
    Davis, Lockyer, 33, 34, 36, 54, 81
    Dodsley, James, 40, 43, 56, 59, 72,
        75, 77, 78
    Dodsley, Robert, 3, 5, 8, 14, 23,
        24, 40, 43, 56, 58, 59, 60, 61, 62,
        72, 75, 77, 78, 81, 96, 97, 98, 99,
        101, 139
    Donaldson, Alexander, 46
    Emonson, James, 14, 96, 98
    Faden, William, 2, 3, 6, 8, 11, 22,
        38, 81, 98, 99, 107, 108, 111
    Field, Thomas, 55, 58
    Fletcher, James (senior), 44
    Franklin, Benjamin, 59, 60
    Frederick, William, 44
    Gardner, Thomas, 8
    Griffiths, Ralph, 1, 8
    Hall, David, 59

Printers, Publishers, and Booksellers
    (contd.)
    Hamilton, Balfour, and Neill, 41
    Henderson, C., 73
    Hett, Richard, 46
    Hooper, Samuel, 71
    Hughs, John, 40
    Innys, William, 3, 96, 97
    Jackson, William, 44
    Jewell (bookseller in Cornwall), 44
    Johnston, William, 67
    Kincaid, Alexander, 46
    Lacy, J., 67, 72
    Leake, James (senior), 44
    Linde, Andreas, 55
    Manby, Richard, 47
    Michell; see: Mitchell, J.
    Millar, Andrew, 5, 36, 42, 48, 56,
        58, 81
    Mitchell, J., 44
    Morgan, J., 44, 64, 65, 69, 70, 81
    Newbery, John, 2, 3, 4, 5, 6, 8, 81,
        96, 97, 98
    Nichols, John, 5, 9, 95, 96, 97, 105
    Osborne, Thomas, 51
    Owen, Edward, 53
    Parker, Sackville, 44
    Payne, John, 3, 4, 46, 81, 98, 99
    Reymers, Charles, 34, 36, 54, 81
    Richardson, J., 2, 3, 11, 13, 14, 15,
        96, 97, 98, 107, 108, 111
    Ruddiman, Thomas (junior) and
        Walter (junior), 50
    Sandby, William, 44, 45, 70, 81
    Sands, Donaldson, Murray, &
        Cochran, 46
    Say, Charles, 12, 13
    Score, Edward (junior), 44
    Scott, John, 56
    Shipton, J., 51
    Shropshire, William, 57, 58
    Spens, Charles, 14, 23, 24, 96, 97,
        99
    Strahan, William, 3, 5, 23, 37, 43,
        49, 58, 75, 76, 77, 96, 98, 99
    Thorn, Barnabas, 44
    Trye, Thomas, 53
    Vaillant, Paul, 38
    White, Benjamin, and Son, 52
    Wilkie, John, 2, 3, 11, 12, 13, 14,
        15, 81, 97, 98, 107, 108, 112

Printers, Publishers, and Booksellers
    (contd.)
  Wilkie, T., 97
  Woodfall, Henry, 65, 73
Prior, James, 8, 105
*Proposal for the Encouragement
    of Seamen to serve more readily . . . ,
    A*, 123, 139
Protest, The, 133
Public Ledger, 2, 3, 4, 8, 98

Quintilian, 39

Rambler, The (by Samuel Johnson),
    3, 4, 8, 128
Ramilles, HMS, 27
Rape of the Lock (by Pope), 89
Rasselas (by Samuel Johnson), 5, 104
Ravaillac, 56
Religio Medici (by Sir Thomas
    Browne), 46
Remarks on Johnson's Life of Milton
    (by Francis Blackburne), 9
Reynolds, Sir Joshua, 103
Richelieu, 114
Robert of Gloucester, 88
Rochester, Earl of, 126
Rolt, Richard, 8, 81, 129, 130
Roper, Derek, 101
Ruffhead, Owen, 23, 31, 71, 103
Russell, Alexander, *The Natural
    History of Aleppo*, 16, 30, 42−43,
    82, 86, 130

Sallust, 38
Sancroft, William, 118, 136
Satirical Review . . . , A, 130
Saxby, Henry, 137
Saxe, Field Marshal Count, 135
Schutze, Godfrey, 56
Shakespeare, Samuel Johnson's
    edition of, 5, 7, 15, 80, 100, 117,
    131
Sharpe, Gregory, 19
Shebbeare, John, *An Appeal to the
    People*, 17, 31, 64−65, 83, 132, 135
Shelburne, Earl of, 49
Sheldon, Father, 44, 69, 70, 131
Sherbo, Arthur, xiii, 18, 104
Sheridan, Thomas, 121, 138
Small, Miriam Rossiter, 127, 129

Smart, Christopher, 3, 5, 8
Smollett, Tobias, 2, 3, 5, 99, 115, 133
*Some Further Particulars in Relation to
    the Case of Admiral Byng*, 17, 31,
    67−68, 87, 132
Spilman, Sir Henry, 85
Spotiswood, John, of Spotiswood,
    50
Stenberg, Theodore, 104
Stevens, Henry N., 60
Straus, Ralph, 96, 99, 101
Student, The, 4
Sully, Maximilien de Béthune, duc de,
    10, 17, 18, 30, 56−58
Swift, Jonathan, 122, 139

Telltruth, Stentor (pseud.), 97
Temple, Launcelot, pseud. of John
    Armstrong, q.v.
Test, The, 14, 23−24, 31, 71, 72, 84,
    112, 114, 132, 134
Thrale, Henry, 103
Todd, William B., 96, 127, 130
Tubingen, 56
Tytler, William, *Historical and Critical
    Enquiry into the Evidence . . .
    against Mary Queen of Scots* (1760),
    reviewed by Samuel Johnson, 22

Ulloa, Don George Juan and Don
    Antonio de, 124, 140
Universal Chronicle, The (1758−60),
    2, 3, 4, 8, 10, 98, 139
Universal Visiter, The (1756), 8, 11, 99,
    129

Virgil, 69, 81
Voltaire, 114

Walesby, Francis P., 104
Walker, the Rev. George, 140
Wallace, Robert, 139
Walpole, Horace, 136
Walpole, Robert, 9, 10, 123
Warton, Joseph (including all references
    to *An Essay on the Writings and
    Genius of Pope*), 4, 16, 29, 39−40,
    81, 82, 88−90, 129
Welch, Saunders, 125, 141
Welsh, Charles, 3, 96, 97
Whalley, Peter, 102, 130

White, Stephen, *Collateral Bee-Boxes*, 19, 29, 35–36, 82, 87, 129
Whitehead, Paul, 68
Whitehead, William, *Elegies, with an Ode to the Tiber*, 24–27, 31, 72, 82, 115, 133
Whytt, Robert, 128
Wilkie, William, 136
Willey, Basil, 105
William of Wykeham, 141

Wilson, Mr., 102, 131
Windsor Forest (by Pope), 89
Wood, Robert, 119, 135
World, The, 112
World Displayed, The, 4
Woty, William, *The Shrubs of Parnassus* (1760), 98–99
Wroth, Lawrence C., 60

Young, Edward, 89